WISDOM
HONOR & HOPE

WISDOM
HONOR & HOPE

THE INNER PATH TO TRUE GREATNESS

Cecil O. Kemp Jr.

Revised Edition

W

The Wisdom Company, Inc.
Franklin, Tennessee

Published by:

THE WISDOM COMPANY, INC.
P.O. Box 681351
Franklin, TN 37068-1351
Telephone: 1-800-728-1145
Fax: 1-615-791-5836
E-Mail: cecil@vol.com

In every applicable instance, the author has personally paraphrased biblical characters, authors and texts in an attempt to make this book more readily understood in modern language. Quotations are not exact.

ISBN 1-893668-00-2
Library of Congress Catalog Card Number 00-105545

To my wife,
Patty

I love you . . . and will throughout eternity.

We are one.
This book is as much your heart and work as mine.

Thank you for your unconditional love
and unwavering support and encouragement.

CONTENTS

FOREWORD

This book is about real and lasting success!

Cecil O. Kemp Jr. gives a clarion call, in *Wisdom Honor & Hope,* to adopt an age-old system of values that have guided the most successful people in history. His teachings are not a get-rich-quick formula or a road map to immediate prosperity in the world. Rather he shares what he has learned through actual experience in the past twenty years, since his renewal and recommitment to what he calls the Philosophy of Wisdom.

This book teaches that intellectual ideals and values, regardless of their philosophical source, are not the beginning point for renewing and transforming our inner spiritual person. Mere intellectual knowledge does not necessarily translate to quality results. Philosophies and creeds mean nothing, Kemp says, until they bring inspiration that equips, empowers and motivates us to live and work in the here and now while achieving our dreams and hopes.

Since the Philosophy of Wisdom is a "working" philosophy, Cecil O. Kemp Jr. endows the words for its most active values with initial capital letters, to remind us of their active importance. Over and over, the author reminds us about the true meaning of success. He quotes from Henry Wadsworth Longfellow's "A Psalm of Life": "Lives of great men all remind us / We can make our lives sublime. / And, departing, leave behind us / Footprints on the sands of time." Throughout the book, the author uses quotes from many ancient, medieval and modern sages, from Aesop to Albert Einstein to Mother Teresa. Their advice in personal and business matters adds credence to Kemp's argument for making decisions based on Wisdom and Truth, a foundation that will endure the test of time.

The emphasis of the book is on our mindset, which is what Kemp calls the inner lens through which we see people, relationships and our responsibilities. It is the inner picture of our heart-held beliefs, principles and values, as seen through the mind's eye in our personal and on-the-job decision making. Kemp asserts that, with the "MindSet of Wisdom," we are assured of making decisions with the most sound judgment and common sense. The MindSet of Wisdom is the byproduct of what Kemp calls the HeartSkill of Wisdom. By choosing to possess the HeartSkill and MindSet of Wisdom, we will find that our lives become blessed with the true marks of greatness: Wisdom, Honor and Hope.

One of the best things about the book is that it teaches how to start over. If you have suffered failure, emptiness, tragedy or crisis, you can begin again. Kemp shows that the beginning point of the right path is inside, where our inner spirit-person (our soul) can possess, and live and work by, Wisdom. This happens with God's help. Kemp quotes the words of the Scottish philosopher Thomas Carlyle: "Out of the lowest depths, there is a path to the loftiest height."

Author Cecil O. Kemp Jr. has been able to distill the ancient values that he has adopted in his own life. With brilliance, insight and a good dose of humor, he relates these to his readers. I wholeheartedly and unreservedly recommend this book to every teenager and every adult man and woman. The author promises his readers: You will be the richer for having read and applied these principles in every role and relationship in your everyday living and working. Even if you are already at the top and consider your life a success, reading this book and applying its Wisdom will move your life *upward* from success—to significance and true greatness.

—Dr. Robert C. Hill, Ph. D.
Oxford Graduate School (USA)

ACKNOWLEDGMENTS

To my Heavenly Father: my most important acknowledgments.

To my mother, Peggy Joyce, and my father, Cecil Sr.
Thanks for the honor of being your son. Your lives and love made a big difference in my life. Cecil Sr.: I feel your tears of joy coming through the holes in the floor of heaven, as you watch over us. Your family misses you dearly and will see you soon. (Save us seats at your favorite fishing spot there.)

Special thanks to:
Rusty and Heather, our children; and their spouses, Tracy and Chris, and their children, Jessi, Justus and one now with God. You all fill our lives with joy.

Jo Ann and Jimmy Dempsey, my older sister and her husband.

Vicky, my younger sister, for your love and for being there every day for our mother, since Big C's death.

Mike and Mary Ann, my younger brother and his wife, for your love.

Uncle John Adcock, for being another wise father figure in my life.

Mrs. Mary Sue Miles, for being a wonderful grade-school teacher.

Coaches Richard Holder and Willis Tullos, for believing in

me and teaching me many wise lessons of life through organized sports.

Ms. Clara Millican and Ms. Dora Medaris, for your prayers and friendship.

Thanks for your enormous contributions to this work to special associates B. J. Rogers, Diana Donovan, Bob Cook, Steve von Hagel and Dr. Robert Hill. Warm thanks to Kathryn Knight for your vast contributions and enhancements to the book. You are a very special person, an extraordinarily enlightened, insightful and passionate soul with a wise, honorable and hopeful heart full of love.

GLOSSARY

THE PHILOSOPHY OF WISDOM

The Philosophy of Wisdom is the viewpoint we hold when a harmonious and interactive partnership with God is the wellspring of our life. It focuses on Divine knowledge, ethic, inspiration and hope and applies these to daily living and working—to shape a life of true greatness that lives up to all its Divinely enhanced potential.

The Philosophy of Wisdom's five core beliefs are:
1. The power source for a life built on the Philosophy of Wisdom is God.
2. True wisdom, purpose and joy come from loving God, listening to God, loving yourself and serving others.
3. We are a combination of the physical and the spiritual, and we must acknowledge and experience *both* to live fully.
4. The life-changing power of prayer is real.
5. We are assured of guidance and help.

The Philosophy of Wisdom's core values and priorities have significance for the here and now—and into eternity. They are:

Faith, honesty and trustworthiness
Justice, responsibility and commitment

Sacrifice, diligence and patience
Discipline, humility and harmony
Faithfulness, courage and peaceableness
Generosity, perseverance and fidelity
Compassion, graciousness and loyalty
Reverence, gentleness and kindness
Wisdom, Honor and Hope

THE INNER PATH TO TRUE GREATNESS

The Inner Path to True Greatness is a chosen walk through life—
traveled by those who allow Divinely inspired faith and vision to
help them grow, mature and fulfill their highest destiny.

WISDOM AND WISDOM TRUTH

Wisdom is Eternal Truth expressed in the Bible and inspired by
God.

Wisdom Truth is something spoken, expressed or discovered
down through history by Spirit-led people of all religions and
schools of thought. It is consistent with the Eternal Truth of the
Bible.

THE MINDSET OF WISDOM

A viewpoint of living and working that upholds eternal values
and recognizes that fulfillment comes from serving others, actively responding to Wisdom's teachings and guidance. Through
the MindSet of Wisdom we begin to see people—their roles,
relationships and responsibilities—through the spiritual lens of
Wisdom, Honor and Hope.

THE SELF-SERVING MINDSET

A viewpoint of living and working that sees the world through
the lens of human knowledge, compromise and empty hope and

is based on materialism, intellectualism, hedonism or another philosophy of folly. The **self-serving mindset** focuses primarily on one's own gain above the needs of others.

WISDOM, HONOR AND HOPE

The three precious inner stones and spiritual blessings of the HeartSkill and MindSet of Wisdom are: Wisdom, Honor and Hope.

Wisdom is highest knowledge. Wisdom's source is God. As the Spirit of God lives and works through a reborn spirit, the truth of Wisdom equips those with the soundest judgment in all choices; it illuminates the actions of their daily life and work.

Honor is highest ethic. Honor takes that Wisdom and habitually puts it into action. Sound character is formed. With Eternal Truth as the inner spirit-person's ethical standard, Honor becomes the interior lifestyle that outwardly is seen as integrity beyond reproach. Honor's administrator is the Spirit of God— alive in a reborn spirit, tutoring and influencing. When Honor thrives in one's life, it takes hold in every personal and work-related role and relationship, yielding excellence.

Hope is highest inspiration. Hope is a Divinely imbued peace and security that allows joy and conviction to reside in the Spirit-led heart—no matter the circumstances, no matter the consequences. It goes beyond optimism. It is a powerful, reassuring "knowledge" in the heart of what is Truth—and of the fact that Truth and Love are abiding. It is a Hope that exists beyond oneself—a Love from the Divine that embraces us all, even those who do not acknowledge and feel its presence. And because it is beyond us, we cannot destroy it or diminish it. It is there, it always has been.

WISDOM'S MOTIVE

Wisdom's motive is unconditional God-like love—love for God, others and self. Unconditional love is the guiding, dominant motive of people who have the Spirit of God inside. This kind of love lets the Spirit of God love through us: It is love based on choice—on an act of will, rather than on feelings or opinions.

WISDOM'S PASSION

Wisdom's passion is the desire to serve God first, others second and self last.

WISDOM'S SELFLESS GRACIOUS-SERVANT PRINCIPLE

This is the core relationship principle of the Philosophy of Wisdom. This principle instructs us to serve the interests of others first and to treat others in relationships precisely as we would want to be treated. Jesus spoke this truth when he said that the person who wants to be leader must first and always be the servant of others. Wise people recognize that we do not exist to be served, but to serve others.

THE SPIRITUAL PRINCIPLE OF CHOICE

The greatest human power is the God-given right of free **choice**. Destiny—now and into eternity—is not a matter of chance, but the result of our choices. When we live and work according to the Philosophy of Wisdom, we make wise choices, which will stand the test of time: Wisdom and the Spirit of God living inside us will direct us. We can clear away the clutter of our inner and physical realities to become selective about our surroundings and incoming messages. Our environment is the feeding ground for our hearts and minds. Our dominant thoughts come from habitually permitting our environment to be a certain way. Whom we associate with, whom we listen to, and whom and what we read are very important and demand that we exercise a high degree of selectivity to make the wisest choices.

THE SPIRITUAL PRINCIPLE OF CONCENTRATION

Concentration on enduring purpose is the key to both temporary and long-term success. Concentration is the act of focusing the inner spirit-person upon a given goal, until ways and means for its realization have been worked out and successfully put into operation or have created a wise habit. To obtain and maintain highest excellence, we must maintain our concentration on proven success methods. Specific ways and means, to a large degree, refer to the habits created by selectivity and concentration and founded on Wisdom and Truth.

THE SPIRITUAL PRINCIPLE OF HABIT

What we repeatedly think in our heart is what we become: this is the spiritual principle of **habit**. What we habitually feed into our heart is our inner spirit-person's food for thought; it is the material from which our character is built.

Wisdom's habits: The dominant thoughts of our hearts are the origin of all our habits. These heart thoughts build and nurture our character, becoming thoughts. These, in turn, become plans and choices, which become actions—repeated over and over again, until they become habits. Wisdom's habits are those that have a heart filled with Wisdom as their wellspring.

THE SPIRITUAL PRINCIPLE OF UNDERSTANDING

We each have particular talents and innermost dreams that become more apparent with the infusion of Divine Wisdom and Truth. When we see with wise, honorable, hopeful eyes, we see not only our own potential but the potential impact and good that our abilities and efforts can bring to others. This realization is the Spirit-induced principle of **understanding**. It is truly an enlightened state that takes us to a higher level of comprehension of the Divinely inspired knowledge and wisdom we possess.

HEARTSMARTS (CORONARY INTELLIGENCE)

HeartSmarts are life's most important lessons learned and retained in the heart of the soul, as the guide for the future. Wisdom instructs us that the heart of the inner spirit-person is the control room of life. The heart is home for our real intelligence and understanding, our inspiration (our hopes, in the form of dreams and expectations) and our spiritual ethical standards.

THE HEARTSKILL OF WISDOM

The HeartSkill of Wisdom is honed by the Divinely-guided spiritual heart, sharpening understanding, perception and insight. Achieving this state of understanding takes a skilled heart—an open, honest heart that seeks and desires this understanding—and acts upon it. With the honed HeartSkill of Wisdom, we are able to upgrade the original source material in our hearts from mere human wisdom, ethic and imagination to the Divine's gifts of Wisdom, Honor and Hope.

With God's HeartSkill of Wisdom inside, there is a huge, supernatural enhancement to the human element, leading to deep heart understanding that does not—and cannot—arise from any other source. This understanding allows for true Hope—a solid foundation and certitude that frees the inner spirit-person to follow the Inner Path to True Greatness without doubts and with conviction.

THE SPIRITUAL PRINCIPLES OF TRANSPLANT, TRANSFORMATION AND INVERSION

Transplant occurs when we receive a new spirit and heart. This takes place at the moment of spiritual rebirth, when the Spirit of God comes to dwell in us and live through us.

Transformation takes place as the Spirit of God changes the mind. We receive a new thinking process, with a new character, built and nurtured by Wisdom and Truth, its values and its principles.

Inversion means turning our old values upside down. Inversion occurs when our inner spirit-person's priorities change from values of folly to the values of Wisdom.

THE PERFECT UNION

At spiritual rebirth, we choose to allow the Spirit of God to come to live in our human spirit.

We are supernaturally transformed: The Spirit of God comes to live inside us, to guide us at work and at home. Our human spirit is joined to the Spirit of God. This is the perfect union.

WISDOM'S AMAZING DISPOSITION

Wisdom's amazing disposition is the mirror image of the Spirit of God living inside those who have been spiritually reborn; it shines out through their lives as gracious goodness. Wisdom's amazing disposition can be seen in a glowing personality and a pleasant, peaceable approach to life. The humility of mind can be seen in selfless, unbiased attitudes, and in just, kind and compassionate actions. Those with Wisdom's amazing disposition command trust, by sharing themselves and their blessings magnanimously and generously with others. They are faithful and diligent, willing to sacrifice, eager to forgive; they are kind, compassionate, just, merciful and patient; they are responsible communicators and possess great self-control.

WISDOM'S POISE

Wisdom's poise is the result of spiritual composure, a calm, balanced approach to life displayed as quiet, gracious and humble confidence.

WISDOM'S PERFECTLY EXCELLENT ACTION

Wisdom's perfectly excellent action is cooperation, for the good of all. It is based on the heart-held belief that cooperation is far superior to competition.

FAMILY CULTURE

According to the Philosophy of Wisdom, the family model is the most effective one for any organization. Under this model, each person is considered equally important, even though each possesses vastly different abilities from the others and has specific responsibilities. The Family Culture model fosters an enduring purpose for an organization. A model built on mutual respect, it creates an environment where commitment to each other—and to common goals—is possible.

SHINING STARS

Within every child lives a soul created by the Divine with un-qualified uniqueness and nearly limitless potential.

As adult mentors, we are called upon to nurture and nourish these Shining Stars, to light them by providing spiritual roots and by equipping them with wings of faith. Then we become a part of the Divine's plan to help new souls soar—to become all God created them to be—pursuing their grandest dreams, fulfilling their spiritual destinies. When we help our Shining Stars to connect at the heart with the Divine, we light small lanterns that can light the world with Wisdom, Honor, Hope, dependability, humility, kindness and love.

PART ONE

Personal HeartSkill

CHAPTER ONE

TWO FLYING RED CARS

THE CAR

WHEN I WAS A SENIOR in high school, I asked my father to buy a candy-apple-red 1967 Chevrolet Super Sport 396 with a black vinyl top and a 4-speed manual transmission. In my mind, *The Car* would be perfect for our family automobile. It was on display at the Brunt-Ward dealership in Louisville, Mississippi, twenty miles from our family's farm in the rural community of Nanih Waiya. After substantial goading from my mother and much begging on my part, my father agreed to drive to Louisville with me to, in his words, "look at a —— car I'll never buy."

We drove onto that car lot in a paid-for blue 1964 Impala and drove off the lot in The Car. My father gave up a car that was paid in full, and financed The Car. I am sure he had to swallow hard that day.

Why did I want The Car? For at least two reasons that seemed important at my teenage level of understanding. First, I was not exactly tall, dark and handsome. The Car seemed to stretch me from five feet eight to over six feet, and it *really* improved my looks. The Car was beautiful and went so fast that it seemed to fly. Consequently, ladies could easily form a distorted perception of its driver's attractiveness. My other reason was similar to the first, but with a slightly different twist. I was sure that, when I drove it, The Car's power and beauty became mine! The Car drew attention to me and gave me worldly status. Every woman living within flying distance of our isolated forty-acre farm knew who I was. Because of the way The Car moved, that circle was one of many, many miles and many, many women!

How I loved The Car! This speed machine not only offered me the opportunity to blow away the cars of my teenage male friends, but also—and I repeat—The Car was a female-attention-getting wonder. It was pretty; it was sleek; it was fast—and the ladies were very attracted by its power and speed. Disguised by The Car as a handsome, charming and daring 115-pound Don Juan, I was very full of myself.

Why would my dad, a wise and highly disciplined man, buy such a car? For one thing, my parents wanted to please me, because they loved me (and my siblings, too) unconditionally. They didn't spoil us, but they lived to serve us. As a parent myself, I have taken what turned out to be unwise actions out of genuine, deep love for our children because I thought at the time they were the right things to do. I have wished many times that I could erase those unwise actions, tear down those misleading "landmarks," and start all over again. Of course, I can't do that. I am sure my parents felt the same way about The Car. When they purchased The Car, using consumer debt, they were trying to demonstrate how much they loved me. Instead, that breakdown of my parents' financial discipline (the only one I can remember ever occurring) became a malevolent landmark for me, an example of unwise action that I followed when I became an adult.

With the 20/20 vision of hindsight, I can see how foolish I was to want The Car and to absorb its characteristics into my self-definition. God's loving favor and protection kept me from having any serious accidents in that first flying red car. But I used The Car, as well as the fact that my parents bought it on credit, to justify my own wrong priorities in buying a *second* flying red car years later. That stupid decision, the result of unwise thinking based on a landmark from my adolescence, had nearly devastating consequences.

THE CAR II

LIKE THE FIRST, the story of that second flying red car is true. The names of the characters, the dates and the essentials have not been altered.

Twenty years later I was driving my current four-wheeled hunk of old steel down Murfreesboro Road on my way to downtown Franklin, Tennessee. I made a horrible mistake.

I looked to my right as I passed the Harpeth Ford dealership. There it was: a candy-apple-red car with a black canvas convertible top and wheels that were nothing short of beautiful. It was in every way as alluring as The Car had been more than twenty years before. My mind and heart leaped from Murfreesboro Road into the Harpeth Ford dealership at the mere sight of this car—and the rest of my body followed. I pulled in. Then I took that black-canvas-topped, candy-apple-red special edition McLaren Mustang for a ride onto the open range.

On my "wild gallop" back to the dealership, I was saying to myself, "Yes, this is the one. I really wa—I mean, *need*—this car." I considered myself to be a financially disciplined grown man. Still, I impulsively bought an expensive and overpowered car, spending nearly fifty thousand dollars on a consumer toy—a racing steed with a huge engine, a supercharger and a nitrous oxide kit that raised the horsepower to well over 500.

Why? (What a silly question!) That car had *power.* Controlling all that power would add to my status. More important, I wanted that car, and I could buy it! My lust for that car overpowered any regard I had for more important priorities in my life. My dominant "want" motives made mincemeat out of any wisdom I might have exercised. The McLaren Mustang assumed the mantle of The Car.

WARNING SIGNS

WHEN I FIRST SAW the red McLaren, I did not procrastinate or dally. I should have used discretion and wisdom that day. But I did not. I acted hastily and thoughtlessly. That's how a foolish person behaves.

Every time I drove The Car, my wife, Patty, reminded me of

my behavior. My response to her concern was always the same: "At least I will die doing something I love." That was an ignorant and stupid thing for me to think and believe, let alone say. My values and priorities in the matter of The Car had become totally skewed.

The Car required a lot of repair work; it seemed something would break every time I drove it. Naturally, I ignored what many would have considered warning signs for me to abandon my idiotic behavior. Instead, each repair job was an opportunity to pack some more horses under that pony's hood.

One evening, Patty and I were returning home from the movies. I thought I would give her a demonstration of how The Car could run when everything was working perfectly—including the nitrous oxide. When I hit the nitrous oxide switch, the car— and, despite seat belts, its unwitting passengers—flew straight up and turned completely around. We landed on the shoulder on the opposite side of the road. Eventually I was able to negotiate the vehicle back onto the highway, but several minutes elapsed before either of us was able to say anything coherent.

Shortly thereafter another incident occurred. Patty accidentally hit the nitrous oxide switch as she went through an intersection, causing The Car to rear up like Trigger and nearly causing what could have been a very serious accident. I finally figured out how wrong my values, priorities and motives were. I decided to donate The Car to our church, in response to our pastor's challenge to sacrifice something we really loved.

LESSONS LEARNED

I THOUGHT I LOVED The Car and I thought I could handle it, spiritually and physically. Let me illustrate how untrue both those assumptions were, how dangerous The Car was and how I endangered not only my life, but also the lives of others.

I took The Car for one last good-bye spin. My excuse for this "power trip" was that I wanted to be sure The Car was in good running condition, since it had just come back from its umpteenth trip to the shop. I needed to check out the mechanical details one last time before I gave The Car to our church. Right?

Wrong!

Close to my home, I passed two men working on the landscape of the entrance to a subdivision. They encouraged me to show them what The Car could do. That's all it took for me to turn back into a cowboy. The little red power machine and I took off across the prairie, nitrous oxide switch on. The Car had fishtailed many, many times before, but never as it did on that crisp December morning. The red tachometer needle rose past 7,000 rpm, and as I tried to regain control, the front passenger-side tire caught some loose gravel at the side of the road. The loose gravel catapulted The Car across the road. As though it were flying out of a slingshot, The Car went airborne. It nicked a tree, creating a whipsaw effect. I found myself four feet in the air, with the tach's needle buried and the nitrous oxide switch on, traveling at well over 200 miles an hour.

The Car slammed head-on into a huge tree. I was knocked unconscious.

When I came to, I was covered with blood and the car was snapped in two. The landscape workers were leaning through what was left of the driver's-side window. One was crying and asking me if I was okay. Although the bone of my skull was showing through a gash in my scalp, I told them I felt fine. I then gave one of the workers my home telephone number so that he could call Patty. Upon request, the other one backed away from the window, allowing me to get out of The Car. I pulled myself out that same window.

The Car looked like a matchstick that had snapped in half. I surveyed the damage to my car while I waited for my wife, who came quickly.

I tried to convince the emergency-room doctor that nothing was wrong with me. The doctor was not so easily convinced. He told me that I had suffered a broken back, one broken wrist, two crushed knees and assorted lacerations and contusions, the largest of which was the canyon-size tear on my forehead. . . . Not to mention the tire tracks across my psyche: The Car was totaled.

I decided to keep The Car's key as a reminder of the consequences of folly. It now serves as the bookmark in my office copy of what I think of as Wisdom's written pages (my Bible), open to the reading that asks the Divine to teach us to number our days, to realize how few they are and spend them as we should.

The church got the insurance check. The junkyard got the remains of The Car. God granted me my life—and a second chance to apply the Philosophy of Wisdom in every aspect of my existence.

These days, I prefer economy-version pickup trucks as my mode of transportation.

☆ ☆ ☆

Bernard Malamud said, "We have two lives. There's the one we learn with and the one we live after that." My challenge to you now is this: Let my experience serve you.

Do you

- go 200 miles per hour in any important facet of your life?
- let money, possessions, power or other false status symbols call your name or divert your attention from your true priorities?
- live your life foolishly and recklessly?
- experience anxiety and fear about events you cannot control?
- have trouble sustaining meaningful relationships with the important people in your life?
- commit foolish actions that put valuable relationships or anyone's life—including your own—at great risk?
- find your life unfulfilling or unsatisfying for reasons you can't define?
- enjoy your life, but feel it could be better somehow?

If the answer to any of these questions is yes, you can benefit immeasurably from what I call the Philosophy of Wisdom.

When you apply the Philosophy of Wisdom to your life, you will begin to follow a wonderful inner spiritual path—a much better path than the one you're on, one with more constructive, more satisfying results.

Choice is an awesome privilege and power force, regardless of how it is exercised. When we choose enduring purposes, true and lasting success will be the result in every aspect of our lives, from the sphere of personal peace and joy, to that of our relationships, to that of leadership wherever we live and work.

Right about now you may be thinking, This Cecil Kemp is one unorthodox dude! Read on, and you'll find that I am one ordinary dude who has had both good and bad experiences and, thank God, who has a lot of healed tire tracks. I followed dead-end philosophies into rock walls and off cliffs. I blindsided myself with folly, compromise and the empty promises of materialism. But almost two decades ago I dusted myself off, turned back onto the right road and, with my family, began again my life's journey along the spiritual path to Wisdom, Honor and Hope. This is the Inner Path to True Greatness.

It may seem strange, at first, even self-important, that the main values in this book are spelled with initial capital letters. There is a reason for this unique typographical style. Many of the words used are commonly understood to be philosophical or theological entities. But I have found that these entities can change your life—and take you on the Inner Path to True Greatness—only when they are actively inspiring you as you live them. To remind you that these values must always be alive in your heart if they are to be beneficial, I have decided to use these caps, in the hope that they will give you a little jolt. For it is that too-common assumption that we already understand, which is the assumption that gets so many of us in trouble. I have also included many nuggets of inspiration, in the hope that some of them will speak to each of you.

The Truth and Wisdom upon which this book is based are backed up with real and lasting results for millions of people over the course of thousands of years of history. If you do not agree with that declaration after you have read this book, if this book does not pay its way in *your* life after you have finished reading it, write to me. I will be glad to give you a full refund of what you paid for *Wisdom, Honor & Hope*.

NUGGET OF INSPIRATION

Let each become all that they were created capable of being.
—Thomas Carlyle

CHAPTER TWO

PRECIOUS INNER STONES

A wise woman who was traveling in the mountains found a precious stone in a stream. The next day she met another traveler who was hungry, and the wise woman opened her bag to share her food. The hungry traveler saw the precious stone and asked the woman to give it to him. She did so without hesitation. The traveler left, rejoicing in his good fortune. He knew the stone was worth enough to give him security for a lifetime.

But a few days later he came back to return the stone to the wise woman. "I've been thinking," he said. "I know how valuable the stone is, but I give it back in the hope you can give me something even more precious. Give me what you have within you that enabled you to give me the stone."

—Author Unknown

THE PHILOSOPHY OF WISDOM

I BELONG TO A GENERATION that was primarily raised on good old-fashioned values and hard work. Our parents' generation inspired us to go out and "conquer" the world! And, like my contemporaries, I set out to do just that—"precious stone in hand." I went to college, excelled and earned more than my father ever had. I had a foundation of my parents' faith and I found that wings lifted me because of their unconditional love. But unlike the man in the tale above, it took fifteen years for the "lightbulb" to go off in my head—and in my heart. It took fifteen years and a roller-coaster ride of materialism, "baby-boomer-itis" and a gnawing emptiness to make me go back and discover what my parents had that allowed them to give so freely, to love and live so assuredly.

I had possessions, wealth and accolades. They had integrity, inner strength and faith.

I had drama, high-energy success and stress. They had laughter, peace and grace.

I had academic degrees, a self-serving mindset, insecurity and doubts. They had Wisdom, Honor and Hope.

Though it took me a long time to go back and rediscover true wealth, I did cash in the three precious stones they had given me. There truly is a successful, time-tested way to run your heart, your life, your decision making and your business. That way creates a satisfying life of significance and meaning.

You won't find it in the so-called precious stone of lots of money. That stone represents mere physical value. You'll find it in the heart and it leads to true abundance, success and inner greatness.

It's a lot more powerful than money or than any red car money can buy.

It's a stone found by making a choice—a heartfelt, soul-stirring choice, not just an intellectual decision. You don't automatically inherit this way of life from wise parents. You don't realize all of its benefits simply by attending church regularly and playing by the rules. It's a big-time, life-changing choice to transform your heart and beliefs and values to a philosophy based on Wisdom and Eternal Truth.

Doesn't sound quite modern enough for today's culture? Are you thinking you'll have to retreat to a monastery in Tibet or a give up all your worldly possessions to live by this philosophy? Think again. This is a decision and a philosophy that puts you right in the middle of life with all its familiar ups and downs, aggravations and joys. No escaping it! You may achieve inner greatness, but you'll still have laundry and bills! You'll gain a sense of awe, and keep your sense of humor! Decisions, problems, pleasures and daily activities don't miraculously disappear, yet making this choice—embracing this philosophy—changes everything.

- It's the easiest choice you'll ever make.
- It's the most difficult choice you'll ever make.
- You can glimpse its power and truth in an instant.
- It will take you an entire lifetime to fully realize its power.
- It not only makes a better person out of you, it makes a better person out of everyone you touch.

THE PHILOSOPHY OF WISDOM'S CORE BELIEFS

The Philosophy of Wisdom holds these five core beliefs—short in number, infinite in scope.

1
THE POWER SOURCE FOR A LIFE BUILT ON THE PHILOSOPHY OF WISDOM IS GOD

We live in a physical world that feels like a seesaw. Everything is always changing, continually playing out the drama of natural beauty and disaster, human discovery, love and conflict, individual or collective sorrow and hope. There is no way to escape it.

Yet there is an unchanging power, an unlimited energy, from which we come. This power is God. This power is full of a Love we cannot fathom. This energy is renewable, forgiving and available at all times. This power gave birth to each of us and enables each of us to sense the one unchanging part of our existence—our connection to the Divine Creator.

2
TRUE WISDOM, PURPOSE AND JOY COME FROM LOVING GOD, LISTENING TO GOD, LOVING YOURSELF AND SERVING OTHERS

This Divine Source of Energy created us, and we are linked to that Source's energy even if we don't acknowledge it. Our deepest dreams, heartfelt passions and natural gifts are the whispers of God's lovingly letting us know that we've got work to do! We were born to work, create and nurture. Our true life's work is to use our talents, what we enjoy doing, to the betterment of others.

Led by Divine guidance, our life patterns change, roads open up, what should make no sense somehow does and, though filled with a sense of work and duty, we begin to experience what some would call the supernatural. It's true!

3
WE ARE A COMBINATION OF THE PHYSICAL AND THE SPIRITUAL, AND WE MUST ACKNOWLEDGE AND EXPERIENCE *BOTH* TO LIVE FULLY

All materiality is fleeting. Possessions are needed because we are physical beings with physical needs—shelter, food, tools and a means of communication—but not because they hold some eternal value. They are a means, not an end. But they *are* a means, sure enough.

A life of inner greatness requires more than a personal fellowship with God and spiritual enlightenment. It requires active participation in the physical realm where he has placed us. This includes abiding by laws and rules that provide for harmony, communication, love and true abundance for everyone. Our day-to-day work, our habits and actions, the character we present to the world and the inner life we build—all are governed by and are a testament to the Philosophy of Wisdom.

4
THE LIFE-CHANGING POWER OF PRAYER IS REAL

Prayer and meditation are not simply a way to ask for things. Prayer is primarily a way to communicate and connect with the Divine and to express gratitude. Prayer recharges the batteries and refocuses vision. Prayer calms the mind and broadens the heart. Prayer requires no physical tools, no academic brilliance, no perfect words, not even a perfect heart. Prayer is a form of surrender to God's influence and wisdom. It is restorative. Only with prayer is it possible to walk with Divine guidance and inner peace and hope.

5
WE ARE ASSURED OF GUIDANCE AND HELP

Teachings, teachers and enlightened souls are all around us. Listen to them! Some are quietly walking in Wisdom, some are trumpeting its virtues, some are humorously extolling its lighter side, some are somberly warning us of great unhappiness without it.

You also have as inspiration and guidance the great teachings and assurances from holy writings. Jesus' teachings, when written, take up less than a tenth of the pages of Socrates', but within His teachings lie the greatest Wisdom and Truth. You have access to His teachings and to the reflections and observations of wise thinkers and adventurous spirits who have dared to walk with Divine Authority. Your walk is your own—your path to inner greatness is the one that you and God create together. Walking in Wisdom can be done and you can do it!

When you embrace the Philosophy of Wisdom, you'll discover some amazing truths:

- Things work out.
- Codes of ethics were developed to enable us to live with more happiness, and not fill us with guilt.
- You'll be more motivated by eternal matters than by temporary or physical matters.
- You won't be free from pain or sorrow, and you will not be above them, but they will not drown you.
- You'll be open to a wealth of inspiration and affirmations.
- You will read, hear and be attuned to the unchanging Wisdom of the ages. You will know when something is connected to Truth. I call this wealth of knowledge and inspiration Wisdom Truth.

So what's all this got to do with successful living and excelling in work and business? Everything, my friend. Everything.

WISDOM vs. HUMANISM

THE PHILOSOPHY OF WISDOM is the viewpoint we have when a harmonious and interactive partnership with God is the wellspring of our life. It focuses on Divine knowledge, ethic, inspiration and hope and on how these are applied to daily living and working, to shape a life of true greatness that lives up to all its Divinely enhanced potential.

One of the critical differences between the Philosophy of Wisdom and most other philosophies of successful living is its source of knowledge, ethics and inspiration. In humanistic philosophies, humans are the source. In the Philosophy of Wisdom, God is the Source. The Philosophy of Wisdom certainly does not ignore or discount the value of the human element—after all, we're here in this physical adventure, aren't we? Rather it understands that our human life is a remarkable tool to experience God's success plan for living.

Compromise or exclusion of spiritual principles and values in our choices is the fountainhead of why money and trappings of material success create so many ills and problems in our culture.

In a *Hagar the Horrible* comic strip, the Old World Viking characters—Hagar; his wife, Helga; and Hagar's right-hand plundering pal, Bud—are enjoying a cup of (something) together. Bud asks Hagar, "If you had your life to live over, what would you do differently?"

Hagar smiles as he thinks about his answer and responds, "I would spend more time pampering and attending to the needs of my one true love."

Mistaking Hagar's meaning, Helga smiles. Bud quickly converts Helga's smile to a frown. He knows exactly what Hagar meant. Bud asks Hagar, "You would do all that for your boat?"

What Hagar's creator, Chris Browne, presents in the comic strip daily are not mere cartoon caricatures. Hagar does portray a true picture of many people in the real world. Sadly, this comic strip portrays what has become normal—foolish, but normal.

Humanistic folly has three twentieth-century philosophical children: materialism, intellectualism and hedonism. Each of these begins with a false premise of the true purpose for our life. Their chief aims are the eternally unimportant. Each is a way of inner being and outward life centered on human values. Materialism places highest values on material well-being and the furtherance of material progress. It manifests as a preoccupation with material things and it places little emphasis on spiritual values. Intellectualism is devotion to the exercise of intellect and human cleverness (human wisdom) or to education and other intellectual pursuits—to the exclusion of Wisdom's spiritual partnership. Hedonism is the belief that pleasure or happiness—on the physical level only—is the sole or chief aim of life.

These philosophies cannot lead to true ultimate happiness or success—which can only be attained in partnership with the Divine within. Because these belief systems exclude spiritual guidance, they lead to a self-serving mindset. This is a dead-end mindset; it places a low priority on the relationships that should be most important to us, treating them like leftovers. This humanistic mindset can lead us to make vows and promises, then break them. Too often, even when we may care, we give far less than we are capable of—or far less than we have promised. Too frequently, consideration of another's best interests—ahead of our own—takes a backseat to things like our egos, personal income and business gains in profits and assets.

The Philosophy of Wisdom is a heartfelt, faith-based approach to life that shapes a person's destiny when that person creates a life in sync with the Divine. That connection is an individual relationship. And since we were created with the freedom to choose, each must choose this relationship.

The Philosophy of Wisdom is not new. In fact, it has been the success formula for people throughout the ages who have lived with a sincere desire to walk with Divine guidance and serve with their gifts. Its proponents and teachers can be found in Scripture and in today's Spirit-led thinkers. But it seems that every generation seems to have to learn it anew. It's not enough to be raised with good values—this certainly helps and aids society—but this alone does not transform a person's life—or a collective mindset.

Why does this outlook, which ought to be so natural for everyone created by God, always have to be reintroduced for every individual and every generation? That's a tough but important question, and I believe it has a multilayer answer. The key explanation lies in our human nature, not our spiritual nature.

Human nature tends to seek the quickest, shortest route despite the teachings of Wisdom. Human nature tends to be self-serving until enlightenment sets in. Human nature tends to turn spiritual guidance into just a list of Do's and Don'ts or religious dogma, and this can turn off people rather than turn on the light of Truth. So the message must continue, although the message does not change: A life empowered by a connection to God leads to the greatest fulfillment, purpose and significance.

☆ ☆ ☆

You might not get all this in one read-through. It may not be a one-trip learning experience. Remember, I had to go through *two* red cars before I let go of the idea that the car had power! But just to get *you* on the right track, I offer a summary of the most powerful philosophy you can embrace:

The Philosophy of Wisdom is the viewpoint we have when a harmonious and interactive partnership with God is the wellspring of our life. It focuses on Divine knowledge, ethic and inspiration, and on how they are applied to daily living and working to shape a life of true greatness that lives up to all its Divinely enhanced potential.

NUGGETS OF INSPIRATION

We cannot teach a person anything, only help them discover it within.
—Galileo

Nothing compares to the promise of your life in partnership with God.
—Cecil O. Kemp Jr.

CHAPTER THREE

MY RACE THROUGH LIFE

If you don't know where you are going, you may end up someplace else.

—Yogi Berra

AND THE RACE WAS ON . . .

I GRADUATED WITH HIGH HONORS from college in 1971 with a degree in accounting. My first job was practicing accounting with Touche Ross, then and now one of the largest public accounting firms in the world. I passed the CPA exam the first time I sat for it.

I left public accounting to become the chief financial officer of a publicly held company at the age of twenty-three. Well before my thirtieth birthday, I was promoted to chief operating officer. At thirty-two, I was proclaimed by the media as a business wonder boy. Read on to see what happened to that reputation in a matter of months. (Notice the word *reputation*.)

During this decade I was in high gear, foot to the floorboard. I was pretentious and preoccupied with chasing symbols of success. I was a walking and talking contradiction; saying one thing and practicing another in my personal and professional relationships and roles . I had limited regard for real character and integrity. Shortcuts up the ladder of success were my specialties. Little did I realize that they would not take me to lasting success.

My family—my wife and children—always remained very important to me (and this was one of my saving graces) but I did not always make it a priority to demonstrate that very real love. I could have been arrested any day during that period of time and justifiably been found guilty of impersonating a wise family and business leader. I had a reputation as a savvy businessperson, even a business marketing and financial whiz, according to some. But the truth is that reputation, inner character and integrity often do not correlate in the business world, or for that matter in many venues.

The money I earned and the status, power and recognition that I had, belied and clouded the reality of what would eventually rise to the surface because of my leadership philosophy, my beliefs, principles, values, mindset and style. My priority was myself, my career was my god, I was consumed by unwise values and dominant desires that resulted from beliefs of folly. These led me to compromise Wisdom, and in some cases, totally ignore and exclude its principles, values and priorities from role, relationship and financial choices.

THE TRIP WAS NOT IMPORTANT—ONLY THE DESTINATION WAS

THERE WAS NO TIME to stop to smell the roses. Certainly no time to plant any rose gardens or nurture the roses. Instead I used people and relationships for my benefit, with little thought that they are the two most important blessings in our personal and business lives. Whenever and however someone could further my career, my ascent up the illusory success ladder, I used them.

I am deeply sorry that I had little true regard for others' welfare or their feelings and opinions. My bottom line was the financial bottom line. This is a view shared by far too many today. "Who can contribute to my welfare?" and "How can this person contribute to my welfare?"are normal business, financial and cultural questions.

At the end of this decade of stupidity, I topped myself by

making some very poor judgments in business. I ignored Wisdom and Truth and followed the dictates of humanism, of my own intellect, cleverness and know-how. I discovered I was not as invincible as I had supposed in my own self-serving mindset.

Equating financial or career success with being a great person is folly. I learned that lesson the hard and very expensive way.

I share this experience to demonstrate how smart I *thought* I was and how full of myself I was! My fundamental mistake during the fifteen years following my high school graduation was that true Wisdom and the right set of priorities did not guide my decision making.

Instead I turned my back on the Philosophy of Wisdom; I left it in the dust, embracing humanistic philosophies that created in me the self-serving mindset. I followed that mindset in my race up the personal and business ladder of blind ambition. Adoption of those philosophies was also the root cause of other failures in both my personal and professional endeavors. I earned hundreds of thousands of dollars in income but saved and planned little. I spent a lot so that I could feel I *belonged* and was *accepted*, and also in order to keep up with those "Joneses"—the people you try to impress by spending money you don't have, even though you don't even know them—or don't like the ones you do know.

How about you? Ever done any of that?

Immoderate and undisciplined behavior helped me accumulate plenty of consumer debt and possessions, but left me spiritually and emotionally bankrupt. See, though we can fool some of the people all of the time, and all of the people some of the time, we cannot fool all the people all the time. As Sir Walter Scott wrote, "Oh, what a tangled web we weave, / When first we practice to deceive!"

MINE IS NOT AN ISOLATED CASE

IN CIVILIZED SOCIETIES all through history, where knowledge and material possessions unwisely became the standards against which success was measured, the inevitable result was destruction in lives, relationships, families, finances and businesses.

Breakdowns have reached high proportions in our modern world because we leave our families—to search for the elusive and illusory success promised by folly via career and the material riches of life. Nearly fifty percent of our children now go to bed at night with only one of their parents in the house the child calls home.

In every corner of the earth, plenty of examples can be found of what happens when we live and work by humanistic folly that denies Truth and thoughtlessly and often ignorantly pretends God either doesn't exist or doesn't matter.

When we mock Divine laws, we only deceive ourselves about the eventual consequences. As Robert Louis Stevenson said, "Sooner or later, we all sit down at the banquet table of consequences." The consequences of handling life, love and money by the principles, values and priorities of folly are broken dreams, hopes, families, relationships, businesses and finances.

When we compromise enduring spiritual principles and values, when we seek to serve self rather than seek first to serve others, we compromise our own happiness. This compromise is known in modern culture as looking out for Number One.

Such selfishness leads to many success barriers with life and finances, because it first leads us to unhealthy emotions and desires, to destructive thoughts, feelings and behaviors. Ultimately, selfishness takes away our inner security. It creates in us discontentment that appeals to our desire to belong and feel accepted. Envy surfaces and that leads us to crave more things. We become pretentious in our attitudes; we spend—and justify borrowing money to spend—to impress people we should not have as our models.

Selfishness sets up other barriers to success—behaviors such as worry and manipulation. It also breeds attitudes like arrogance and rebellion that lead to ill-advised decisions and poor results in our relationships and with money.

I chased the pot of gold at the end of the illusory rainbow of the unimportant. Maybe you too have discovered that those alluring and pretty promises yield a meaningless pot empty of spiritual, emotional and financial gold.

INSTANT PUDDING

IN ANOTHER *Hagar the Horrible* comic strip, Hagar and his buddies are shown climbing the ladder up the side of the castle of a neighboring queen and king, plundering victims. The queen dispenses the king, Sir Edmund, to the roof in order to determine what the clamor is all about. Just as Hagar reaches the top rung of the ladder and is about to step onto the roof, from inside the castle the queen yells, "Sir Edmund, who's out there?" Looking snobbishly down at Hagar, in an apparently arrogant tone of voice Sir Edmund says, "Just another social climber, dear!"

Social climbing is no joke. It has become a destructive way of viewing and pursuing success. It feeds on self-doubt and causes people to make decisions based on instant "wants" rather than long-term needs.

We live in an instant-pudding culture that favors instant results and measures success by immediate results. The best movie is the one that earned the most at the box office *this weekend*. The best salesman is the one making the biggest sales *this week*. As soon as we have a job, we immediately want to feel and look successful—we buy beyond our current means for instant "prosperity." We want what others have and we want it *now*!

Wanting another's advantages is too often the spark that lights the fire of determination to get them, any way we can. Wanting money, status, esteem and power have become the accepted norms of society. Our expectation is that our lives will continue to get better, easier and marked by possessions.

At every turn we are conditioned to be discontented with what we have. Our expectations are no longer to be content with anything about our life. We are taught that chasing things is the proper way to satisfy our emptiness and our deep passions for significance, recognition and accomplishment.

Blind ambition is never contented. And chronic discontentment is a dangerous approach to life, career and money. It leads to greediness and a self-serving mindset, making us susceptible to doing really dumb things that are highly destructive to ourselves and those we influence.

I was so determined to grow, grow, grow, that I led my family and its businesses on debt binges! In the businesses, we used millions of dollars in debt to fund "instant" rapid expansion at a time when we were generating huge cash profits (multiple millions) but I was not prepared when (a) interest rates climbed to almost 20 percent, and (b) we did not have people resources to support rapid expansion.

The self-serving mindset is never content and is always, always looking to expand. The blind spots in the self-serving mindset are the costs and risks of choices. With this mindset, we lose the ability to prudently assess future scenarios that might result from current choices.

And then we wake up one morning and find ourselves raking through the ashes of our lives. In less than six months, a business I had committed my life to *and sold my soul for*, fell to pieces. It had to be sold off in bits and pieces. Collectively, the selling prices equaled less than the proverbial song.

BACKWARD TO GO FORWARD

I WAS FACED, AT THAT TIME, with some very pointed questions. I was blessed to have been raised by parents who had given me spiritual and ethical roots from which I could draw inner strength—if I admitted to the truths that, deep down, I knew held validity and wisdom.

I found a story about a rich and powerful farmer who looked at barns full of material wealth and arrogantly ordered employees to tear them down.

Just as I had, the farmer told employees to build new, bigger ones to hold more material wealth. This was what he ordered one day from death, though at the time he did not know death was lurking around the corner.

My similar behavior marked the beginning of quite a long time of reaping from the bad soil and seeds I had sown and farmed. Afterward, I sat at home, unemployed, and I whined and mused aloud, "What happened? Where did it all go?" Even then, I still had the self-serving mindset. My dominant thought was, "What am I going to do?"

Because of me, my family had virtually no savings and no income.

Most of our fair-weather friends had disappeared into thin air.

This was indeed a very sobering period in my life. But I did have plenty of soaking time, for introspection and inner inspection.

I finally woke up and, with a new heart, retraced my steps to the entrance onto the path to Wisdom and Truth.

I finally realized the truth that intellectual, material and other human values do not buy or lead to prosperity, true happiness, peace of mind or spiritual well-being. I finally understood with deep sadness and remorse how far I had fallen from what I had been taught by my parents about true happiness and integrity. I realized that when we make choices, we need to make ones that will *stand the test of time*, not simply satisfy the selfish, momentary desires we all face in everyday living and working— which later will be discovered to be nothing but a lot of unfulfilling baloney!

Yes, philosophies of humanism did lead me to great short-term results when measured as many incorrectly measure success. But these flawed philosophies and the self-serving mindset led me, as they have millions of others, to chase imaginary rainbows. A rainbow's end, of course, cannot be found. Only fool's gold sits waiting for rainbow chasers. I dead-ended with a feeling of financial, emotional and spiritual emptiness. For me, the search for a pot of gold held near-disastrous consequences.

EVERYTHING THAT GLITTERS IS NOT REAL GOLD

WE LIVE IN A HIGH-TECH, fast-paced and extremely busy society. We can't slow down enough to catch up with ourselves. Often we are so busy chasing things, we haven't taken the time to understand or learn why.

For over a half century now, there has been a steady decline of individual and societal ethics and a decline in quality of personal and professional relationships. Time-honored hallmarks in the lives of people, families and organizations—truth, fairness, equity, gratitude and benevolence—have become distant memories to millions, as they did with me in the 1970s. This is because of individual choices to live and work by humanistic, nonsensical and high-sounding philosophies of folly, rather than the sound and commonsense philosophy of living by Wisdom and Truth.

A BETTER WAY

IT DOES NOT HAVE TO BE this way. There is a much better way, a path in life that leads to much better and truly lasting results. I call it the Inner Path to True Greatness. In 1982 I made a choice of conscience to go backward and consciously establish an enduring foundation; from there I moved forward again, but this time on the a better path, pursuing what has lasting value for others and for myself.

Consider this story from Daniel Woglemuth, received by way of internet e-mail from a friend of mine:

After three years of intense use, my laptop computer at the office quit operating. I worked with our in-house technician to diagnose the problem and discovered that it wasn't going to be worth the expense or effort to refurbish it. His final suggestion was to order a new machine.

We had been ordering our laptops from the same manufacturer for over three years. Even so, I was surprised by what I discovered on Friday when I picked up my new machine. As I lifted the screen and plunked away on the keyboard, I was astounded at the familiarity. The design, layout, appearance and touch were nearly identical to the model I had just retired. I had expected a noticeable change; after all, a span of three years in the world of technology is enormous.

Nonetheless, I was grateful to once again have a reliable system, so I gathered my new carrying case and ancillary computer paraphernalia and went back to work.

Now, several days since the switch, I realize how inaccurate my preliminary assessment was. Storage space, operational speed, communication tools and performance are profoundly different. It hasn't taken me long to appreciate what research, engineering and innovation have achieved in the last three years.

The transformation may have been initially obscured by familiar packaging, but what appearance denied, usage exposed. This is a remarkably different machine.

Change, at the core, needs to be at the core. Different packaging without different contents incites initial enthusiasm, but quickly disappoints.

This week at our house, my wife celebrates (theoretically) another birthday.

What I've learned over the past twenty-plus birthdays is that her packaging hasn't changed much. She's taken wonderful care of herself, and works to maintain a similar look year to year. Yet she's remarkably different from the woman I married. A difference that's internal, personal, powerful and delightful. She works at growing and changing year in and year out, and it's a change at the core.

My replacement laptop computer provided the perfect reminder of what real change is all about. Internal change is more subtle than external changes, but it's also more valuable.

People who make a difference start on the inside. They invest in the things that change and enhance their being, and they let time reveal what appearance hides. Same look and feel, but profoundly different and more wonderful at the core.

There are always choices of philosophy to embrace and shape our decision making and our actions. The enlightened soul (inner spirit-person) traverses the high way; the blind soul takes the low way; and the rest of the searching souls drift back and forth.

When we choose philosophies other than the heartfelt, faith-based Philosophy of Wisdom to guide our choices, the rewards are temporary, easy feel-goods that leave spiritual and emotional emptiness lurking around the corner. Saint James taught that status, power and money are like grass and flowers; they wither and fall, but Wisdom and Truth are forever. Englishman Charles Spurgeon also said it right: "It is not how much we have, but how much we enjoy that makes happiness." So did

Marquis De Condorcet, a French philosopher, who wrote, "To find contentment, enjoy your own life without comparing it with that of another."

It took reconnection to the Divine and allowing the Spirit of God to guide me, to restore my inner being to the state needed for me to move forward securely and confidently, with a truly lasting inner foundation.

I adopted Wisdom's age-old system of principles and values for everyday living and working. It has worked for millions down through history. Some have been history's most successful and famous. Most were like me, far less famous. Yet both groups have enjoyed remarkable success and significance within their everyday living and working worlds.

I was blessed, in that I had wonderful examples to follow. I was given unconditional love, the hope of a bright future, a format to follow, a set of spiritual guidelines to live by and models of true success to emulate. I had these twenty years before, when I set out to conquer the world. But I did not realize their value until I was farther down my chosen path of folly. I finally saw the wisdom in the old adage from Aesop, "The desire for imaginary benefits often involves loss of present blessings."

NUGGET OF INSPIRATION

The Inner Path to True Greatness is a chosen walk through life—traveled by those who allow Divinely inspired faith and vision to help them grow, mature and fulfill their highest purpose and destiny.

CHAPTER FOUR

ROOTS AND WINGS

*Eden is that old-fashioned House we dwell in every day
without suspecting our abode, until we drive away.*
—Emily Dickinson

I believe it was Mark Twain who in essence once said, "When you turn sixteen, you think your parents are the dumbest people on the face of the earth. When you turn twenty-one, it's amazing what they learned in only five years." It took me a bit longer than five years, but when Truth hit, it opened my eyes and heart to the simplicity and power of my parents' beliefs and values—what I had thought were outdated principles.

A SLICE OF MY STORY . . .

MY PARENTS, Peggy Joyce and Cecil Sr. (Big C to his children), held strong beliefs that created and nurtured in them the models of principles, values, priorities, motives and thinking necessary for wise decisions in life. That is true because they lived and worked by the Philosophy of Wisdom—which places the spiritual connection to God at the center of thought, emotion and decision making. Their inner power source was Wisdom, Honor and Hope. Their life's passion was serving others.

Beyond words, in their actions and inaction, my father and mother expressed a genuine love and deep respect for each other, their four children and all others. This love and respect were always evident, displayed by the twinkle in their eyes and the joy on their faces.

My parents' virtues included honesty, courage, perseverance, faith, sacrifice, self-discipline, responsibility, fidelity and loyalty. They lived with justice and compassion. They worked hard, always sought the truth, never shirked their duty or forgot their friendships. My parents respected their employer and friends, always giving above what was expected or required. They were respectful of all and, though always eager and willing to help, never intruded. Both practiced a strong work ethic. They were easily the hardest workers I have known.

They were not driven by greed or desire to accumulate excessive money for themselves or spend money on themselves; rather they were motivated to be a blessing to others. With their time, skill and money, they were givers, not takers. Without fanfare, they often used those God-given blessings to do kind things for those who could not do for themselves. They knew that Love helps those who cannot help themselves.

When they made a promise, they kept it. Their character and integrity manifested quietly every day. They let conduct do the talking. Ben Franklin could have been describing them when he said, "Well done is better than well said."

Their character, discipline and minds worked together to make them persons with great inner prudence and discretion in all dealings. One of the facets of my dad's personality that impressed me most was mentioned by one of his sons-in-law at my dad's funeral: it was dad's ability to reduce something to its lowest common denominator. His genius for essentials made him a very wise thinker. His wise heart controlled his mind and thinking.

They taught their children well. They did not pay us for picking cotton grown on our farm, or for doing our chores. They felt these tasks presented opportunities for my siblings and me to learn responsibility and accountability. They believed there were lessons within the work that provided a reward better than money, namely: helping others as we sought to do our best.

Big C and Peg demanded our best from each of us kids. Excuses were not in their vocabulary. Excellence was the only standard by which they measured themselves—and us. Yet they instilled confidence by example and nurtured it with constant encouragement.

KEEP IT SIMPLE

MY PARENTS' CORE BELIEFS were reflected not only in how they treated others, but in how they treated their finances.

They were savers. They first set aside a percentage of every dollar earned, before any of the household income was spent.

They avoided debt. They didn't use installment accounts, credit cards or any form of debt to buy consumable goods and services. Even when they had to use debt to buy an appreciating investment asset like a home, they paid the debt as soon as possible. They wanted the peace of mind and the interest of savings! They paid off their home mortgage in thirteen years!

They were prepared. Sometimes I think my parents invented details. They were always advance-preparation addicts and the most skilled planners I've ever known.

These simple but very profound and powerful positive life and money habits of my parents created powerful financial results, allowing my father and mother to retire when he was fifty and she was forty. For over a quarter of a century after that, they remained financially free to do what they wanted, whenever they wanted.

There will be scoffers who may guffaw about my parents' lessons, saying they're not applicable in today's high-tech, fast-paced world. Few would deny that their qualities would be good models for our personal lives—but models for workplace behavior and for money management? Consider the undercurrents giving rise to those questions.

We have come to the point in society, especially with material resources, where pretentiousness, shallowness and selfishness cause us to overlook the beauty and enduring value of simplicity. Thus we incorrectly attribute success only to those who seem remarkable when measured by standards of quantity of dollars, possessions and intellect. We have a superficial and false perception of real success. We incorrectly think success can be achieved only by "superpersons" who are more charismatic, visionary, creative or skilled physically or mentally than the ordinary person could ever be.

Yet my parents—two very ordinary people—were lit with inner greatness and I consider them two of the most successful and prosperous people I've ever known. They were at peace with God, their work and their actions. They loved, laughed and added to the lives they touched. They were financially sound and spiritually centered. They were successful. Period.

Were they millionaires? No.

Were they famous? No.

Were they so religious that they were granted superhuman ability to withstand the discipline of sacrifice? I think they'd get a good-natured laugh at that one!

And were they perfect? No.

With my mother's permission, I share a very human element of my upbringing.

WE'RE ALL PART OF THE HUMAN FABRIC

SOMEHOW, WITH ALL OUR FAULTS, foibles and imperfections, our Divine connection to God can still weave us into His beautiful fabric of blanketing grace. We can always join in on the Grand Plan and turn our lives into a meaningful experience.

My father was certainly not perfect.

Like so many others in our culture, and so many others throughout human history, my dad loved liquor—sometimes seemingly more than he loved his family. The family tree on his side featured a very long line of heavy drinkers. He was the type who went on drinking binges that entailed disappearing for weeks, and suddenly reappearing. As he came through the front door of our small farm home, he was always carrying some olive branch—flowers or some other gift of appeasement for Mom, and a sack of hard candy, perhaps, for us kids.

He was never verbally or physically abusive to anyone during or after his whiskey binges. See, he was a happy man who got happier when drunk.

Too much liquor dulled his normally wise thinking capacity, so he had a false perception. He thought there was nothing wrong with heavy drinking or leaving us in the lurch for weeks at a time.

This weakness persisted in my father's life until the day my mother and I found him in jail in a little town about fifty miles from our farm. After paying the family's hard-earned money— to bail him out of a situation created by his choice to waste even more hard-earned money—and after being worried "half to death," Mom and I laid the law down. Before taking him home, there in the parking lot, we both told him in no uncertain terms to quit drinking or we were leaving and would not reappear.

My mother's years of loyalty, forgiveness and unconditional love paid off. In an amazing display of self-will and discipline, my dad changed that day. To my knowledge, he never drank heavily or disappeared again. But do you know what truly impressed me more than my dad's transformation?

Actually there were two things that impressed me most about this experience.

First, my mother's incredible willingness to forgive and have faith in a less-than-perfect man. That's not a humanist decision, folks. That's from a heart that believes in Love. One simple soul helped another, and together they experienced all of life—ups, downs, joys, pain, God's grace and God's leadership.

Second, my father proved what it really means for a husband to truly love his wife. Somehow, love finds a way. My dad lived what Theodore Hesburgh said, "The most important thing a father can do for his children is to love their mother." Of all his many invaluable lessons, seeing my father's unwavering love of, and faithfulness to, my mother was perhaps his best.

So, Cecil Jr., do a few imperfections in your parents and a childhood where money was tight explain your turn down the path of folly?

No a million times.

Because of my parents' love, devotion and sacrifice, my three siblings and I were spiritually enriched beyond measure and, in the material sense, never lacked for anything truly needed. We knew that true wealth, riches and prosperity are wise states of heart and mind. Those most important life lessons were also reinforced by wise relatives, teachers and coaches, some mentioned in the book's Acknowledgments. These and other wonderful relatives and mentors made up what I call my Family Culture, an indispensable element of society.

Let me be clear.

My own personal choices—to turn away from the values and priorities of highest Truth seen in my parental models—explain why I hit the wall in 1982. While it is very true that many people are reared in dysfunctional families, there still is the real hope of Truth—and claiming it begins by taking that first step of personal choice to change.

No imperfections can stand in your way of achieving inner greatness if you walk with Divine guidance. No imperfections in your parents, your mentors, yourself or your culture. You think you've got great excuses for being mediocre instead of great? Okay—write them all down, and then crumple that paper up and toss it away. Be done with it.

Get on with living and loving—and changing, if you've got to.

My dad did.

I did.

You can.

Here's how.

NUGGET OF INSPIRATION

High expectations are the key to everything.

—Sam Walton

CHAPTER FIVE

SPIRITUAL KNOWLEDGE

Wisdom is the breath of the Divine's power, a pure influence flowing from the glory of the Almighty.

If we keep doing things the same old way, we will keep getting the same results. Wisdom offers us a way to break out of that dead-end pattern and take a new path. *Being* great precedes *doing* great. Being our best starts inside each of us with the transformation of our inner spirit-person, through Wisdom. Nothing is impossible if we take the high road of wise choices, conforming our actions, ways and means to the beliefs, principles and values of Wisdom.

THE HEARTSKILL OF WISDOM

NATURAL INTELLECT and educational attainments have their places in our lives, but they do not provide a firm spiritual foundation for wise thought and action. A higher quality of life depends not on IQ, educational level or cleverness, but rather on a spiritually wise heart. A heart with the HeartSkill of Wisdom creates the MindSet of Wisdom, so that choices are based on eternal principles.

You need to believe in and follow a philosophy for living that works. This philosophy is one that places God's influence and eternal know-how at the center of the heart. This philosophy places greatest value on servitude and love. This is the Philosophy of Wisdom.

Wisdom's benefits include the exchange of complexity for simplicity, of inner conflict and distress for true peace, of illusions and imitations for true and lasting success. Living Wisdom yields genuine happiness, as we are inspired and motivated in our everyday living and working by life's highest source of inspiration. We have within us genuine enthusiasm for life and a source of energy that allows us to run without being weary. We have the power, passion and skill within to soar to new heights, lifted on inner spiritual wings.

Solomon taught that Wisdom is the material we must use to build a successful family or business. By understanding and applying Wisdom correctly, our homes and businesses will be filled with precious and pleasant riches. In a very real way, Wisdom is the mortar that holds together the bricks of our families, our businesses and our individual lives. Solomon also said that if we possess Wisdom, we will give good advice, have common sense, have inner strength, be discerning and prudent in thought and choice, be esteemed and honored for being honorable, have firmness of purpose because we have the stability of wise character and the Spirit of God living within us.

THE SEARCH FOR WISDOM AND TRUTH

ONE COMMON ATTRIBUTE of truly wise and successful people is their ability to determine the truth and then make decisions based only on Truth. Since deception is so rampant in our society, we should always make Truth the object of our quest.

For most people, the body of wisdom knowledge is composed of wise teachings from parents and other mentors, along with life experiences. Besides my parents and specific life experiences, the most comprehensive and reliable body of knowledge about Wisdom that I have found is the Bible. Throughout *Wisdom Honor & Hope* I refer to biblical wisdom as Wisdom with a capital *W*. Someone who does not believe in the Bible's perfection as I do will probably still agree that it is a better guide than any philosophy of folly. Therefore I recommend the Bible as the supreme source for decision making in every aspect of life.

The huge difference between Wisdom and other positive philosophies is that Wisdom begins with enduring purpose: *being* rather than *doing*. In the course of being, Wisdom directs our doing, which creates truly lasting benefits for ourselves and everyone we influence. Saint Augustine told us that to wisdom belongs understanding of eternal things; to knowledge, the rational understanding of temporal things.

TAP INTO WISDOM TRUTH

I ALSO QUOTE the wisdom of many ancient, medieval and modern philosophers whose teachings are consistent with the true Wisdom. Biblical teachings of Jesus and Old and New Testament prophets, together with these wise words and guidance that ring with eternal values, love and truth I call Wisdom Truth. This is not a finite body of knowledge—but a Divine source of inspiration that connects us all.

Wisdom Truth is the wealth of knowledge underlying the Philosophy of Wisdom—a unifying Wisdom, Eternal Truth and the work of the Divine Creator. It has inspired a vast source of affirmations you will find as your heart and mind are open to Divine fellowship and to leading a life of significance. You will find yourself reading a profound quote that lifts your spirits and makes you say, "Aha! That is Truth! That is Wisdom!" And that is Wisdom Truth—a connection to a unifying Wisdom that links us all, despite distance in miles or centuries, despite differences in culture, ethnicity or religion. The words and thoughts and works of art that other Spirit-led people leave for us lovingly tell us we are not alone—guidance and support is all around us. Besides being sprinkled throughout this book, some of these words are also offered in the Appendix. Wisdom Truth buoys the heart and reveals the potential of all humankind.

True Wisdom begins
- with the realization that the material world has no value in the long run;
- with the realization that life is a gift;
- with gratitude and respect for this gift;
- with gratitude and respect for the Giver;
- with gratitude and respect for all other life;
- when one decides to emulate givers and not merely have a hand held out for receiving.

Ultimate wisdom and greatness begins with the realization—through a lifetime of study, a moment of blinding enlightenment, a period of soulful, reflective prayer—that the greatest giver we can emulate is the Divine Creator.

YOU'VE GOT TO BELIEVE!

TO POSSESS WISDOM is more than an intellectual achievement or the accumulation of knowledge. It is the *expression* of that knowledge in our attitude and conduct toward everyone with whom we come in contact, in every part of our lives. In short: Wisdom is knowing what is right and doing it.

In order to stay on Wisdom's path and live with significance, you've got to believe in the Truth of your philosophy. You may experience loss, doubts, confusion and conflicting emotions throughout life, but your firm core beliefs will sustain you.

You must believe with all your heart the Philosophy of Wisdom's core beliefs:

1. The power source for a life built on the Philosophy of Wisdom is God.
2. True wisdom, purpose and joy come from loving God, listening to God, loving yourself and serving others.
3. We are a combination of the physical and the spiritual, and we must acknowledge and experience *both* to live fully.
4. The life-changing power of prayer is real.
5. We are assured of guidance and help.

It won't work if you practice a religious life and leave out prayer and communion with God. It won't work if you follow all the man-made rules and then wait to see if God infuses you with inspiration, direction and inner greatness. If being a do-gooder makes you feel great inside but you lack a relationship with the Divine . . . don't kid yourself! That great feeling may simply be a pomposity of pride, a self-righteousness that is often paired with a judgmental attitude toward others. The only way to make a lasting and eternally meaningful difference with your life is to become a human embodiment of God's Spirit and plan. You've got to believe that this is your destiny, your purpose and your source of greatness. You've got to believe!

And once you believe, your life begins to change.

BUILD YOUR LIFE ON WHAT YOU BELIEVE!

JESUS TAUGHT THAT WE CAN BUILD a house on one of two foundations, rock or sand. The house built on rock endures through all storms; the house built on sand will be washed away. The house of the parable is a symbol of our lives, as well as of our families, relationships and businesses. The sand can be seen as a symbol for folly. Rock, then, stands for the wise way of God. We choose which one will be our foundation. Without the proper foundation, we will surely never achieve the truly important and eternal purpose God has for our lives.

YOUR FOUNDATION—CORE BELIEFS, PRINCIPLES AND VALUES

ALL MINDSETS—all approaches to life—begin with beliefs and values, the core building materials of our choices. All personal, relationship and leadership philosophies are based on a body of fundamental beliefs felt to be true by those who embrace and practice the philosophy. Our beliefs and values order the priorities of our lives. People who do not live and work according to what they say they believe *do not believe* what they say they believe. Our values, priorities, motives and desires are interdependent elements within an intricate system of the mind: of thinking, decision making and action.

Belief—a firm conviction you have about someone or something—is one of the most powerful forces in your life. Core beliefs are those that shape all other beliefs that you hold. These core beliefs will determine how you view situations and decide what is "true" about what you experience. They also shape your principles—or fundamental rules of conduct—which determine your actions, reactions and habits. These are the beliefs and principles upon which our philosophical foundations are built and stand or fall. We view them as enduring and unchanging over time.

Our values are what we feel in our hearts to be important—or what we treasure. We create priorities by choosing what we value most.

There are four fundamental categories of values:

1
ME VALUES

Me values include ego gratification, status, self-importance, achievement, survival, pleasure and self-indulgence. Me values feed motives such as greed and self-preservation at any cost. Me values create a self-serving mindset that directs one's actions toward the service of selfish desires. Me values characterize the priorities of materialism, hedonism and other philosophies of folly.

2
SPIRITUAL AND MORAL VALUES

Spiritual and moral values may be rooted in religion, social custom, parents' teachings or general cultural views. They can be very important in achieving success and excellence, depending on their foundational beliefs. Ordinary human moral values and Wisdom's spiritual values are not the same, do not have the same source and yield significantly different results.

3
MATES' VALUES

Mates' values are group values. Combined with spiritual and moral values, they are among the most important values of Wisdom. Relationships are tightened or torn apart, depending on whether the interaction between mates' values and spiritual and moral values is a positive or a negative one. The desire to belong, which is prominent in mates' values, can be a constructive desire, or it can create inner obsessions that lead to harmful, even destructive, compulsive behavior. An excessive need to belong or be accepted can be the hidden motive for unwise priorities.

4
HUMAN VALUES

Ordinary human values develop in response to issues such as the general welfare of the earth and of humankind, for example, people have values about ecology, pollution and concern over nuclear power. While these issues are important, they are mutable and ever changing, and so are the values that grow from them. They are not fertile ground for the development of eternal and unchanging values of Wisdom.

DEVELOP A WISE HEART

THE CONTENT OF YOUR heart controls your decisions, not just the content of your mind. A spiritually wise heart, therefore, is the most important ingredient in making wise decisions in our daily living and working.

What you value reveals what's in your heart—your true nature. Do you value money? Physical beauty? Prestige? Business acumen? Academic honors? When your core beliefs and principles are in line with Wisdom, your values will change from the material and the temporary to inner qualities and the eternal.

You can tell when a person is on the Inner Path to True Greatness. That person reflects Divine Wisdom and values what is truly important: love, honesty and trustworthiness; justice, sacrifice and diligence; discipline, responsibility and commitment; faithfulness, loyalty and fidelity; patience, gentleness and kindness; compassion, humility and graciousness; peace, harmony and generosity; courage, perseverance and faith; Wisdom, Honor and Hope.

When you weave these values into your inner spirit life, their qualities will become the qualities you manifest in your outer life. Your entire being will glow with a radiant, positive, genuine and caring personality—what I call Wisdom's amazing disposition that manifests outwardly as gracious goodness!

WINGS OF AN EAGLE

DO YOU REMEMBER in one of the *Star Wars* movies when Luke Skywalker is retracing his lineage? He finds he has descended from a great warrior. He asks his mentor, Yoda, why he too is not a great warrior. Yoda tells him that the secret to being a great warrior (Jedi knight) is the Force inside him. Then Luke asks his mentor to help him bring the Force within him to life. Yoda tells Luke to cover his eyes. The blindfold prevents Luke from relying on what he can see with his eyes. He has to trust what is inside him to be his guide.

I believe that every decision we make should be considered through the eyes of the Spirit of God. From the private inner room of our soul where He lives, we should allow the Spirit of God to teach us and guide us. Reflective meditation and earnest prayer to God for insight and affirmation help us to discern Wisdom and Truth. Wisdom says, *Put on your blindfold! Trust the Spirit of God inside you!* Wisdom teaches us that the Spirit of God comes to live inside us when we are spiritually reborn. At spiritual rebirth, we are supernaturally transformed. The Spirit of God comes to live inside us to guide us at home and at work. This reborn inner spirit-person has the wings of an eagle and is a skilled expert at all of life.

THE HEARTSKILL AND MINDSET OF
WISDOM = ACTION

ALL PHILOSOPHICAL APPROACHES propose a way of being inside that dictates a mode of action and predicts results in the way we believe—and behave. The state of being inside, regardless of the philosophical source, manifests itself on the outside. In fact, beliefs alone—beliefs unlived—accomplish nothing. *There must be a union with the beliefs so complete that the believer is compelled to act.* A philosophy without a believer to take action is a dead philosophy, nothing more than a worthless and powerless ideal or value.

The Philosophy of Wisdom is much more than believing—it is an active participation in life. It calls for action, not simply meditation. It trains the heart and mind to see with Divine eyes and creates the HeartSkill and MindSet of Wisdom—a viewpoint of living and working that upholds eternal values and recognizes that fulfillment comes from serving others, actively responding to Wisdom's teachings and guidance.

When we choose to be guided and directed by the Spirit of God and Divine Wisdom, the inner HeartSkill and MindSet of Wisdom show clearly as gracious goodness in our everyday living and working. Our character, habits, knowledge, ethics, zeal and enthusiasm, our thoughts, skills, personality, disposition, attitudes, motives and passions all emulate God's. Then, and only then, can we achieve the highest and lasting excellence in our personal, family and professional roles and relationships.

THE BEST IS YET TO BE

THERE'S A LOT TO BE SAID for the phrase *Your life is what you make of it.* I believe, however, there's even more truth in this statement: *Your life is what you and God make of it together.*

If you believe you were destined to simply slip through this physical adventure leading a mediocre life that neither goes against the status quo nor places you at any risk, then that's probably what you'll experience. If you believe that your destiny is to succeed in accumulating as many possessions as possible, then that may very well come to pass. If you believe that your destiny is to suffer disappointment and put up with less than what you dream for yourself, then unfortunately . . . that may manifest itself in your life.

But if you believe that your destiny is to live intentionally and unexhaustedly toward becoming the best person you can be, using your talents and gifts; if you believe that your destiny is to become part of the miraculous work that touches and changes the world for the better; if you believe that it's not only okay but *essential* to fulfill your dreams and your Divine-led destiny; then you will live a life very few experience but all can claim . . . if only they believe.

TODAY IS THE FIRST DAY . . .

WHERE YOU ARE RIGHT NOW does not need to be where you are headed tomorrow. One of the greatest things about claiming your destiny as a co-pathblazer with God is that you only have to change what is inside *you* to start. You're the greatest tool God has to help shape your destiny. He has already placed magnificent abilities within you that He's able to tap into!

Destiny is not a matter of chance, but of choice—the greatest human freedom. You can choose to travel blindly in search of self-gratification, or you can choose to be guided by a Divinely inspired heart. Let your heart choose your paths in life and be guided by the compass of Truth.

So how to start down this path to inner greatness? This destiny of greatness? You've got to clear your head and heart of the nonsense you've learned from humanistic beliefs that place value on selfish gain and temporary pleasure. You've got to acknowledge that the dreams, talents and innermost drives that are part of your nature can become part of the Divine Spirit's energy that shapes the world, the community, the family and yourself. You've got to become a leader, which means you've got to develop a servant's heart.

You've got to: Claim it. Believe it. Live it.

NUGGET OF INSPIRATION

Wisdom is the precious inner cornerstone of the path to excellence and lasting success. It magnifies our talents and illuminates the path of life. In its right hand is long life and in its left, riches and honor.

—Cecil O. Kemp Jr.

CHAPTER SIX

SPIRITUAL ETHIC

As we think in our heart, so we are.

—(personal paraphrase of) Solomon

LIVING YOUR BELIEFS AND SHAPING AN HONORABLE LIFE

WHEN YOU LIVE ACCORDING to the Wisdom imparted to you and through you, you live with Honor—an old-fashioned word with powerful, eternal relevance. Honor is the second precious inner stone and blessing that comes with following the Philosophy of Wisdom. The first is Wisdom itself.

Honor takes that Wisdom and habitually puts it into action. Sound character is formed. With Eternal Truth as the inner spirit-person's ethical standard, Honor becomes the interior lifestyle that outwardly is seen as integrity beyond reproach. Honor's administrator is the Spirit of God—alive in a reborn spirit, tutoring and influencing. When Honor thrives in those lives, it takes hold in every personal and work-related role and relationship, yielding excellence.

Abiding in Wisdom and committing to Honor leads to the third precious inner stone and blessing—Hope. Hope is God shining through you and your work. Hope lifts you and sustains you and at the same time lifts and sustains others. The confidence, security and assurance you possess, by walking in faith with the God of Hope, activates your current and future dreams and expectations—and illuminates, blesses and motivates others to seek this Light. All three blessings work together to take you down the Inner Path to True Greatness.

Traveling the Inner Path to True Greatness is your highest destiny. And as contradictory as it may sound in a culture that promotes materialistic success and celebrity, true greatness comes from serving. *Yes, serving!* Serving God and serving all that God loves and cherishes. Yet so very few—even very few of those who claim sincere belief in God—ever walk this incredible path. Why?

SETTING YOUR HEART AND MIND TO GREATNESS

I BELIEVE THAT WHAT GETS in our way of true greatness is small thinking. We let our physical experiences—our routines, daily grinds, sudden traumas and to-do lists—fill up our thoughts. We think these temporary concerns are huge. And, you know, they *are* huge when that's all that fills our mind and heart. But in the eternal scope of a spiritually aware heart, these are so small compared with the magnitude of our true calling and duty. Being a part of that Divine plan does not bring daily grinds to a halt, but it sure helps us differentiate between small thinking and big thinking!

The ultimate in small thinking is to focus only on oneself! When we focus only on ourselves, our situation, our status, our wants, our finances and our physical desires, we cannot help but ultimately feel empty and unfulfilled. This is the focus of the self-serving mindset that leads to dead end upon dead end, to folly, loss of hope and low self-esteem. For, you see, your focus reveals what you value and look to for self-worth. Focus on yourself, and you end up relying on one small gear in the great creation of life. Focus on the Divine, and you focus on the entire grand, miraculous Creator and creation itself—allowing the small gear that is *you* to become part of that wonder and plan.

This is the MindSet of Wisdom, which opens your eyes, heart and life to eternal realities and values—a MindSet that leads to peace, self-worth, fulfillment, true greatness and Honor.

YOUR THOUGHTS SHAPE YOUR DESTINY

WHAT YOU VALUE and how you prioritize those values will determine how you ultimately think. What you think becomes how you act. And as Charles Reade so wisely wrote:

> *Sow an act, and you reap a habit.*
> *Sow a habit, and you reap a character.*
> *Sow a character, and you reap a destiny.*

Do you see, then, that what you put into your heart and what you think about will shape your destiny? Living a life of Honor begins with how your heart responds to events around you, to your own desires, to your very thoughts. This is why your beliefs and values must be clear in your heart and mind. This is why a life of true greatness must begin with Wisdom before it can become Honorable and create Hope for others. This is why Saint Paul wrote to the Philippians what I paraphrase here:

> *Whatsoever things are true,*
> *whatsoever things are honest,*
> *whatsoever things are just,*
> *whatsoever things are pure,*
> *whatsoever things are lovely,*
> *whatsoever things are of good report;*
> *if there be any virtue and if there be any praise,*
> *think on these things.*

It's so easy to try to skip over working on the inner you, isn't it? It seems easier just to do good deeds and try to demonstrate love and charity when these actions benefit our situation or when guilt settles in, from time to time. We rely on old patterns of thought that lead to patterns of behavior we may not be particularly proud to own. Worse yet, we often shut down the thinking process; we ignore our conscience and resort to the self-serving mindset. Our character and integrity become a little more flawed each time our mind reaches an unjustified conclusion—rationalizing a self-serving decision, making an unwise choice in the moment of truth. Folly subordinates the heart to the mind. Eventually, our purpose and vision refocus away from what is truly important because our inner spirit-person changes. This explains why people keep making the same mistakes over and over. It also explains the importance of rising to a new and higher way of thinking.

Wisdom teaches us that we are what is in our hearts; Wisdom inspires us to think and make choices according to good hearts. Wisdom's principles, values and skills must fill our hearts. Setting our minds to the MindSet of Wisdom, which serves others, first requires the HeartSkill of Wisdom. This HeartSkill is acquired through great effort and, in this whirlwind culture, that effort takes much discipline and faith. A life of Honor begins in the heart, and only then does it come from the mind.

The way we think affects our emotions, our ability to relate to others and our ability to cope with difficult circumstances. Psychology maintains that positive, accurate, effective thinking increases happiness and success in life. Positive thinking *is* good for you, but this premise of psychology fails in its focus on the sufficiency of human willpower and know-how. Positive thinking alone cannot provide a firm foundation for wise decision making.

Gaining a heart guided by Wisdom requires more than mere human effort. Those whose hearts and minds have not been spiritually refocused by the Divine Spirit will eventually find that, despite their positive, accurate or effective thinking, and attempts at self-control and discipline, they are ultimately powerless to combat the negative desires in their hearts and the unfortunate impact of their thinking and actions. The residual, flawed condition of the heart will inevitably manifest itself in unwise thoughts, in attitudes of mind, in words and deeds.

This is why we must begin with Wisdom and absolute trust and love for that which is greater than ourselves. We cannot achieve true greatness, success and Honor on our own. We cannot focus our heart and mind on the spiritual and the eternal without embracing and being embraced by Divine Light and Truth. Without this faith and belief, we're left with our own motives, wills and desires to try to find fulfillment—and that's not a winning plan.

THE HEART OF THE MATTER

OUR CHOICES AND ACTIONS in roles and relationships are most influenced by the level of our HeartSkill. HeartSkill reflects our dominant motives and deepest desires. A motive is the reason we do something. Motive operates on the human will through an emotion or a desire seeking to cause the will to act.

The four principal humanistic motives are:

Safety—concern for self-preservation; desire for health, food, shelter, clothing and financial security; desire for comfort and peace of mind;

Greed—excessive desire for intangible and tangible things, including safety, love, esteem, recognition, power, money and possessions;

Love—desire to please and to provide for wants and needs; object of desire can be self, family, friends, God or idols;

Esteem—desire to be recognized; desire for prestige; desire for power, success, luxury and accomplishment.

Unwise motives are based on excessive desire. When acted on, an excessive desire often leads to destructive consequences, sooner or later. Greed, for example, is never a wise motive for any thought, choice or action. Greed, and love of self or idols, are the root motives of the overactive emotions, feelings and desires that characterize the self-serving mindset.

With this self-serving mindset, we can have a deeper desire to win than we do to serve. In that case our means (way) will be aimed at doing whatever it takes to win. Too often, the desire to win is so deep that the morality of the means we use to compete becomes unimportant; we disregard the consequences of our actions in the blind pursuit of victory. This is a classic example of the self-serving mindset under the influence of deep-rooted unskilled heart material (desire to win), which leads to compromise in choices and actions. The Greek philosopher Aristotle put it succinctly when he said that he counted the man who overcomes his desires as braver than the one who conquers his enemies, for the hardest victory is the one over self.

We can learn to live by Wisdom's motive. We can develop a deeper desire to serve than to win for ourselves. We need only to follow the Philosophy of Wisdom.

WISDOM'S PASSION

WISDOM'S METHOD of ensuring that wise desires are manifested is cooperation. Wisdom's perfectly excellent action is cooperation, for the good of all. It is based on the heart-held belief that cooperation is far superior to competition. Wisdom teaches us that our capability to attain something by using any means available does not justify harming others.

Wisdom's passion means that Wisdom guides our inner spirit-person in such a way that our deepest desire becomes to serve others—God first, then our neighbor—before self.

We all come to many forks in destiny's road: the road of Wisdom leads to excellence; the road of folly leads to grave and troubling consequences. When we deeply want something, good or bad, we generally find a way to achieve it or obtain it. Obstacles don't seem to matter when our desire is deep enough. Depth of desire orders our motives into two separate lines marked "more dominant" and "less dominant."

Normally, the more-dominant-motive lineup is distinctly shorter. Don't confuse short with less powerful or unimportant. There is nothing wrong with deep desire, regardless of its emotional source (sentiment, affection or passion), if—and only if—that deep desire leads us toward enduring purpose.

"BUT I REALLY *NEED* THIS . . ."

UNWISE MOTIVES often rear their ugly heads when we allow our emotions to confuse needs and wants. When wants are perceived as needs, we seek to have them no matter what the consequences for ourselves and others. Any action taken in response to a motive or desire not subordinated to Wisdom's motive (unconditional love) and Wisdom's passion (desire to serve) will likely lead to unwise choices with bad consequences.

Wisdom's definition of needs and wants is quite different from those found in the flawed philosophies of folly and the self-serving mindset. Wisdom teaches us to think of *needs* as those things necessary for our survival, and *wants* as whatever we desire to improve our comfort and our satisfaction.

World-renowned Russian writer Leo Tolstoy wrote a story titled "How Much Land Does a Man Require?" Tolstoy portrayed the devil offering a peasant all the land the peasant could walk around in a single day, from sunrise to sunset. Tolstoy's peasant, in response to the devil, pushed himself mercilessly. The peasant's greed, his excessive love of self, his all-consuming desire for personal well-being and prestige impelled him to walk a very wide circle. His effort was so great that, at sunset, the peasant collapsed and died.

Ask yourself how the peasant expected to benefit from his deal with the devil. Was it worth it to gain a large estate at the cost of his soul? This question deserves serious consideration.

Most of us realize that good consequences are the pleasant fruit of making levelheaded choices based on highest beliefs, principles and values. These highest beliefs, principles and values order our priorities through wise motives and controlled desires. Bad consequences result from unwise choices, based on deep and excessive desires. Our desires, more than any other component of the inner spirit-person, rule our hearts and greatly affect and influence our mindsets and thinking.

The spiritual principles of choice, concentration and habit are critical to building the bridge of HeartSkill from the self-serving mindset to the MindSet of Wisdom.

THE SPIRITUAL PRINCIPLE OF CHOICE

You always do what you want to do. This is true in every act. You may say you had to do something, or that you were forced to, but actually, whatever you do, you do by choice. Only you have the power to choose for yourself.
—W. Clement Stone

The greatest human power is the God-given right of free choice. The choices we make in response to situations always determine our destinies—on and off the job, and into eternity. Sometimes we can only choose our attitude toward a disaster, but our destinies do result from choices, whether of thought or of effective action.

Choices ultimately lead to actions with consequences. Choice is the most important dynamic of the Philosophy of Wisdom—and also, unfortunately, of the philosophies of folly.

When we live and work according to the Philosophy of Wisdom, we make wise choices that stand the test of time. Wisdom and the Spirit of God living inside us will direct us.

Sow Choices, Harvest Consequences

OUR LIFE IS THE SUM TOTAL of our choices. Our choices are the result of our inner beliefs, principles and values, which flow from our inner spirit-person's source of inspiration and order of priorities. This explains the importance of always considering both the short-term and long-term consequences of our choices.

Author George Eliot labeled choice "the strongest principle for growth." I agree. By our choices we select the soil of our souls, we plant seeds therein, we water and cultivate the soil and the seeds and, ultimately, harvest the consequences of our choices. To further demonstrate the awesome power of choice, consider the following seven important choices all of us make at one time or another during our lives:

1. We choose who and what we believe.
2. We choose who and what we value.
3. We choose how we will treat others.
4. We choose to love or hate.
5. We choose to cooperate or compete.
6. We choose our employers.
7. We choose to act with integrity or to compromise it.

Every single person has this power to choose. This power cannot be taken away from us. We choose to be who we are and do what we do. We can be who we want to be and do whatever we choose. So who we are and what we do are direct results of our choices. We can literally alter our lives by choosing our attitudes. Our mental attitudes are established by our heart's beliefs, principles and values. Wisdom teaches us that as we think in our hearts, so we are. Choice is not controlled by our minds, but by our hearts. The quality of our choices reflects the quality of our heart's condition—wise or unwise.

Every day we are confronted with unremitting pressure to choose from competing alternatives. We have many choices of things to do, places to go and routes to get there. We have many choices of vocation and recreation. This is true in both our personal and our business roles and relationships. Amid the clamor of all these appeals for our energy and attention, we must learn to exercise a high degree of selectivity.

We need to realize the importance of being selective about our surroundings because our environment is the feeding ground for our hearts and minds. Our dominant thoughts come from habitually permitting our environment to be a certain way. Whom we associate with, whom we listen to and what we read are very important; they demand that we exercise a high degree of selectivity. Our environment comprises the sources that influence us through our five senses. What we repeatedly think in our hearts is what we become: This is the law of the Spirit. What we habitually feed our hearts is our inner spirit-person's food for thought; it is the material from which our character is built.

The complexity—and brevity—of our lives make it imperative that we understand and apply the spiritual principle of choice. Our life spans are not long enough to do everything they want to do. True, with the pace and liberality of society and our tendency to be self-focused, we can get an awful lot of living done in a much shorter time frame than our parents could. Still, to accomplish anything worthwhile, each of us must be wisely selective, discriminating in favor of essentials and forgetting trifles. We do not have a limitless capacity to experiment. The irrevocability of many of the decisions we make on a daily basis also motivates us to search for the wisdom of selectivity.

Spiritual Wellness

AS WE MAKE CHOICES and act on them, our inner spirit-person is not only making choices, but also changing into something different from what it was before the choices were made. Sometimes these choices change our inner spirit-person into someone wiser. At other times, when we compromise Wisdom, the opposite happens.

The quality of our inner spirit-person is constantly progressing or regressing, as the consequences of our choices register on our mental, emotional and spiritual memory banks. With Wisdom inside, our inner spirit-person possesses the highest quality mental, emotional and spiritual inspiration, knowledge, skill, power and passion. Joy, peace, freedom and happiness result for us and for everyone in our sphere of influence when our inner spirit-person follows Wisdom in choices and actions. Moving in a wise spiritual direction leads to peace and to knowledge. We develop a greater ability to understand, and we do so with greater clarity.

On the other hand, our inner spirit-person can ignore Wisdom and be inspired and guided by folly. Here the inner spirit-person regresses and becomes the kind of person who is unwise, devoid of true knowledge, powerless, without true love and highest passion. When folly is the choice of our inner spirit-person, we and those around us experience lack of joy, restlessness, discontentment, bondage to material success and its trappings, overall unhappiness both inside and out. This is a major indication that philosophies of folly are always destructive, no matter how attractive they may appear on the surface. When we go in an unwise spiritual direction, we are not capable of understanding our own spiritual and moral flaws and we can act in a dishonest, destructive or otherwise morally reprehensible fashion without feeling the slightest guilt or hesitation. We surrender to the self-serving mindset.

Conscience and Choice

WHEN OUR INNER SPIRIT-PERSON'S beliefs, principles, values and priorities are Wisdom's, the law inside us will tell us to do the wise thing, even though our instincts and human desires might tell us to ignore our inner law. When our heart ingredients are founded on a philosophy of folly, then the law inside will tell the inner spirit-person to make choices that seek self first, over Wisdom's better demands that others' interests be our priority and passion.

Our conscience causes us to recognize our obligations. Our conscience makes us feel guilty or triggers mental, emotional and spiritual pain when we are unwise in our choices and behavior. If we had no inner sense of right and wrong, or needed no such thing, or if there were no absolute right and wrong, then there would be no basis for accusing anyone of wrong conduct. When we program our conscience by the principles of the philosophies of folly, or we ignore the internal guide of Wisdom, we can make huge mistakes in role and relationship decisions. This is because the instincts and desires that rule us under the influence of folly are little more than raw emotions. Instincts and desires know no right or wrong.

It is not enough just to listen to conscience. We must also respond wisely. An unwise response to our conscience will lead to unwise choices that can result in terrible consequences. When we fail to keep our inner voice tuned to Wisdom's principles, or when we ignore the voice even though it is well tuned to Wisdom, we begin to build a wall around our conscience. This leads to blocking its sensitivity and our receptivity. Our conscience can then become weak and ineffectual, causing us to blame other people, the business community or our institutions for problems that Wisdom would attribute to our individual choices. The source of individual problems can be traced directly back to our choices, if we follow a decision model that either excludes or compromises Wisdom's spiritual values.

Make the Difference

RECENTLY, THE *Wall Street Journal* reported a poll that found that Americans felt the decline in moral values to be the number one problem they currently faced. The *Journal* commented that many of those polled blamed the decline in moral values on failures of the institutions of religion and law enforcement to function satisfactorily in our society. Many of you will agree that moral decline is among the most significant problems we face to-day, if not the most significant.

Let's take responsibility and quit placing blame anywhere except squarely on our individual shoulders. The decline in moral values has not been institutionally created. These and related problems happen at and exist at the individual level. It's time for us to stand up and take individual responsibility for the destructive influences of folly. This means we need to do something personally to change, so that the spiritual and emotional well-being of others become our real priority.

Try this exercise: Pretend you have just learned that you have one year to live. Consider living your next year as though it were your last chance to always see the value in every person, even those whom some may label as throwaways. See the beauty within them, and stretch out your hand to help them. Keep everything in perspective, including self-importance. Look for the opportunity to serve rather than be self-serving. Believe that every enemy is a potential friend who is one reconciling conversation away. Let these wise choices inspire you to take individual responsibility for the challenges faced by our society today, always letting your conscience be guided by Wisdom.

THE SPIRITUAL PRINCIPLE OF CONCENTRATION

CONCENTRATION ON ENDURING PURPOSE is the key to both temporary and long-term success. Concentration is the act of focusing the inner spirit-person upon a given goal until the means for its realization have been worked out, whether the goal is for some successful business operation or to acquire a wise habit. To obtain and maintain highest excellence, we must maintain our concentration on proven success methods. Specific ways and means, to a large degree, refer to the habits created by good choices and concentration and founded on Wisdom and Truth.

Maintaining concentration means controlling self-attention. Two of the greatest benefits in practice of the spiritual principle of concentration are unity and commitment to mission. These are outward indications of inner spiritual peace and serenity.

Wisdom tells us that our inner and outer persons must be

harmonious if we are to attain and maintain highest excellence in our personal and business roles and responsibilities. When our inner spirit-person's concentration is divided between self and others' interests, unity and commitment to mission will not be possible in a family or a business. When that happens, everyone with whom we come in contact is affected. To move in the direction of being others-focused rather than self-focused, we must first take control of our emotions, feelings, desires, instincts, motives and thoughts. We can choose to practice the spiritual principle of concentration and turn our efforts in the direction of Wisdom.

Very briefly, the way to do that is to acquire a wise heart, one possessing the HeartSkill of Wisdom. When we have a wise heart, the mind follows a system of decision making that has the Philosophy of Wisdom and its beliefs, truths, principles and values at the foundation of every choice and action. With Wisdom inside us shaping our character and integrity, Honor commands an others-first caregiving strategy that, with repetition, becomes a habit.

THE SPIRITUAL PRINCIPLE OF HABIT

WE GET HOOKED by the tyranny of the telephone ringing. Then there are the demands of the appointment book. If these two aren't enough to stress our systems, then there's the apprehension that grips us inside when we look at the calendar. So much to accomplish. Not enough time. No time left at all even to figure out what is really important, much less to do those things.

We placate ourselves with the thought, "Oh well, there's always tomorrow to change," as off to sleep for a few hours we go.

Then the alarm clock goes off. We either throw it across the room or hit the snooze button twenty times. Then back on the treadmill! Doing the same things the same old way, and getting the same old so-so results. We're hooked on busyness, on unimportant activity.

Too often, those of us in leadership roles cause people and relationships to stand in line at a closed door while we attend the ringing telephone. Or we are off and running to the next appointment without a backward glance. Or we are so stressed over the calendar that we scream through the closed door, "Now is not a good time. Pleeeeeeeeease come back later!"

We are all creatures of habit. Habits are behavior patterns that grow out of our thinking (in the heart first) and lead to our doing something in the same way, repetitiously, over and over again. When we don't create our habits according to Wisdom, we always feel tired, beat, stressed out, anxious to the max and afraid. And when we're alone, we feel our emotional and spiritual tank is totally stone-cold empty! Eventually we must all face this question: what habits do we choose to cultivate? We can choose the habits of folly or the habits of Wisdom.

Habit: Servant or Slavedriver?

HABIT CAN BE A WONDERFUL SERVANT or an awful master. The very best habit in life is focusing your concentration on others first, giving care and serving their needs and best interests as you would want to be cared for and served if the roles were reversed. Making habit your servant in that fashion can only be accomplished from the MindSet of Wisdom. Inversely, if yours is the self-serving mindset, your habits will enslave you to your selfish interests. The habits of selfishness and self-service persist because they offer some form of satisfaction.

The deceitful self-serving mindset and the cleverness of folly can fulfill our selfish interests. They will also fabricate an outward personality and disposition suitable to that momentary need. That counterfeiting of the real person we are inside will eventually lead to significant negative consequences at home and on the job.

Sow an act, and you reap a habit . . .

A WISE HEART establishes the MindSet of Wisdom through the spirit principle of habit. Thoughts lead to plans; plans are executed in actions and choices; actions and choices form habits; habits determine character; the choices that determine character fix our destinies.

While Wisdom is power, knowledge by itself is not enough.

To be useful, Wisdom must be applied correctly. Despite the many rewards of getting and applying Wisdom, my experience and observations lead me to warn you that even people who know what is wise do not always act accordingly. It is a grievous error to assume that those who know the most will act the best. Naive trust in the efficacy of knowledge is just that—naive. Once we understand this idea, we should strive to act in the ways taught by Wisdom, to do the right thing. By right, I mean we will serve and be caregivers to others. Our priority and passion will always be to treat others exactly as we would want to be treated, if our roles were reversed. A truly wise person makes it a habit to express Wisdom, not simply with words, but in his or her attitudes and conduct.

To begin to move toward that as your everyday living and working reality, you must first understand why whatever is currently the focus of your concentration *is* the focus. You must understand the beliefs, principles, values, emotions, feelings, desires, instincts, motives and thinking that led to the creation of your everyday living and working habits. If your habits are founded in Wisdom, the objects of your concentration will be desirable. If your habits are founded in folly, the objects of your concentration will remain undesirable. The power of habit is pervasive; it can be a negative or a positive influence on your life, depending on where and how your habits originated. Habit is an important dynamic that works in concert with choice, regardless of whether the underlying philosophy is Wisdom or folly.

The principles and values of any philosophy become effective in our everyday living and working only when these literally become the fabric of our whole being. Habitually applying principles and being guided by values create and weave the fabric of our inner character. Inspired foundational truths, habitually applied, become the soul and substance of our person. Through habitually applying Wisdom's inspired truths, our inner spirit-person becomes a mirror image of our inspirational source. Then we will not have to stop in the middle of a personal or business decision to question what is wise or unwise. We will know the right thing to do.

A LIFE OF HONOR

We first make our habits, and then our habits make us.
—John Dryden

Sow a habit, and you reap a character . . .

YOUR LIFE IS A SELF-PORTRAIT of the philosophy and habits you choose for daily living and working. Your character is presented in your habits and actions. The manner in which you *care,* the manner in which you *act,* the manner in which you *err*—these reveal your character.

Character—the manner in which you *care*

CHARACTER BEGINS IN THE HEART. What you care about—your values, your beliefs, your personal priorities—will determine your actions, reactions and decisions. The honorable heart cares deeply about remaining connected to the Divine through prayer, meditation and reflection. The honorable heart is motivated by Wisdom's passion—to care about and care for (serve) others. The honorable heart reveals its Divine source of inspiration by seeking to do what is just, wise and compassionate in all matters.

One cannot shape a legacy of Honor based on upright character without honestly caring about our own spiritual walk, the welfare of others and doing what is right in all matters. This can only be achieved by continually turning inward to distill, reflect, evaluate—and commune, in the private inner room of our soul, with the Divine Spirit waiting there for us.

Character—the manner in which you *act*

YOUR TRUE NATURE is revealed by how you demonstrate what you care about—your values and beliefs. You can choose wise habits that will lead you toward wise actions. Sit quietly and think in your heart about your habits and your actions. Do they reflect your beliefs?

You believe in God—do you pray?

You believe in justice—do you speak up?

You value friendship and family—do you take the time to let loved ones know?

You care about being a force for change—do your day-to-day manners reflect this?

Alex Hamilton said that those who stand for nothing fall for anything. If we discard our convictions about truth, we become totally vulnerable to folly. We can be sidetracked into unwise actions at any point in our journey. We are left with a losing hand. Our highest aspirations are blocked from view. Sooner or later we learn harsh, expensive lessons and painfully discover that folly's promises lead only to illusions, false success symbols and fool's gold.

Your belief system should dictate your lifestyle, not vice versa.

Honor and Choice

WE KID OURSELVES if we say we are victims of circumstances. The truth is, we all choose our direction and, thus, are cocreators of our lives. The course we chart is dependent on our inner creation, our outer representation and our ability to grow. No lottery win, no lucky break, no physical change can endow us with a noble, confident spirit. This comes only from sincere dedication to enduring purpose and direction.

Character—the manner in which you *err*

FORGIVING ANOTHER PERSON is difficult. Forgiving yourself can seem impossible! Remember that no one is immune from making mistakes. We all take wrong turns, defend information that later proves to be untrue, make decisions we later regret.

The true test of character is not a tally of a person's mistakes. Rather it is the manner in which mistakes are handled—admitting an error, recognizing how the error was made and committing to change how the error was handled. Handled honestly and honorably, errors teach us, mold us, strengthen us and enable us humbly to teach others.

The path of Truth and a life of character do not travel along a straight line. There is a constant doubling back to reconsider, rethink and learn new things about yourself, your spiritual walk and your association with others. Think of a mistake you have made. Remember how you handled that mistake. Ask yourself if your actions were wise or unwise. Forgive yourself for making the error and commit yourself, with Hope, to taking the wise and honorable path. Then consider Bernard Malamud's comment: "We have two lives. There is the one we learn with and the one we live after that."

Sow a character, and you reap a destiny!

A man's character is his fate.

—Heraclitus

There is at least one thing far better than making a living and having lots of money and possessions—*making a life.*

Your character and reputation for honesty and integrity, in both belief and action, are more valuable than money, possessions, educated know-how or skills. In the end, we are left with what we've made of our lives. Did we dare to live out our dreams and convictions, or did we merely strive for security? Do you want to measure your life against a true standard? Then look into your heart to see how Honor and character act as true measures of real achievement.

We must not set our aspirations, goals and priorities by what others value and find desirable. Changing who we are and how we see on the inside will bring about the right outward behavior—not vice versa.

So stop now, take a breath, begin to begin again—and answer truthfully to yourself: What must I do differently—starting today—to create lasting benefits for others and myself whose lives I influence and impact each day? What must I do differently, starting today, to begin living a life of Honor?

As you reflect on those questions, consider the following story, a paraphrase of the country-music song "Chain of Love," written by Johnny Barnett and Rory Lee, performed by artist Clay Walker.

> *He almost did not see the older lady stranded on the side of the road. But in the dim light at sundown, he could see she needed help, so he pulled up in front of her Mercedes-Benz and got out. His Pontiac was still sputtering when he approached her. Despite the smile on his face, she was worried,*

wondering whether he would hurt her. He didn't look trust-
worthy. He looked poor and hungry. He could see that she
was frightened, standing out in the cold. He knew how she
felt, that chill that fear puts in you. He said, "I'm here to help
you, ma'am. Why don't you wait in the car where it's warm?
By the way, my name is Joe."

It was only a flat tire, but for an elderly lady that was
enough. Joe crawled under the car, looking for a place to put
the jack, skinning his knuckles badly. Soon the tire was
changed. As he tightened the lug nuts, she rolled down the
window and began to talk to him.

She told him she was from St. Louis, just passing through,
and she kept thanking him for coming to her aid. Joe just
smiled as he closed her trunk. She asked him how much she
owed him. She was thinking any amount would have been
fine with her. To him this was not a job and helping someone
in need was normal—God knows there were plenty who had
given him a hand in the past. He had lived his entire life this
way, and it never occurred to him to act any other way. He
told her that if she really wanted to pay him back, the next
time she saw someone who needed help, she could give that
person the assistance they needed and she could, Joe added,
"Think of me."

He waited while she started the car and drove off. Though
it had been a cold and depressing day, Joe felt good as he
headed for home.

The lady watched in her rearview mirror as he disap-
peared in the twilight.

A few miles down the road, the lady saw a small café and
went in to grab a bite to eat and take the chill off. It was a
scene totally unfamiliar to her, a dingy-looking place. Out-
side, there were two old rusty gas pumps and inside, the cash
register was like the telephone of an out-of-work actor—it
didn't ring much.

Her waitress came over and brought a clean towel to
wipe her wet hair. She had a sweet smile, one that even being
on her feet for the whole day could not erase. The lady no-
ticed the waitress was surely ready to give birth to a child, but

she never let the strain and aches change her attitude. The lady wondered how someone with so little could be so giving to a complete stranger. Then she remembered Joe.

After the lady finished her meal, and the waitress went to get change for her hundred-dollar bill, the lady slipped right out the door. She was gone by the time the waitress came back. The waitress wondered where the lady could be, then noticed something written on the napkin under which were four more hundred dollar bills. Tears welled up in her eyes as she read, "You don't owe me anything. I have been there too. Somebody once helped me out, the way I'm helping you. If you really want to pay me back, do this: Do not let this chain of love end with you."

That night when she climbed into bed, the waitress was thinking about the money and what the lady had written. How could the lady have known how much she and her husband needed money? With the baby due next month, it was going to be hard. She knew how worried her husband was. As he lay sleeping next to her, she gave him a soft kiss and whispered, "Everything is gonna be all right. I love you, Joe."

Life's a circle. The seeds we sow come back to us. That's why one who lives life well says to others, "Take my hand. Stand on my shoulders. You are my brother and sister and, together, we can."

Such people make a deliberate choice to openly express their love, knowing they are blessed to have the opportunities to nurture others. And each experience fills their heart deeper with love and compassion that makes their world a far better place, one safer and more secure for all.

Live your true destiny! Let your character shine from within with Divine Light. Let your life become a vehicle for Hope!

NUGGET OF INSPIRATION

This is the true joy of life: being used for a purpose recognized in yourself as a mighty one!

—George Bernard Shaw

CHAPTER SEVEN

SPIRITUAL INSPIRATION

Of all the forces that make for a better world, none is so indispensable, none so powerful, as hope. Without hope men are half alive. With hope they think and dream and work.
—Charles Sawyer

In the cries of the anguished—there is Hope. In the heart of every stirring soul—there is Hope. In the dreams that keep us looking up—there is hope. In the dawn of a new day—there is Hope. In the sanctuary of prayer, in the connection to the Divine, in the eyes of a child—there is . . . and always will be . . . Hope.

I WILL LIFT MY EYES . . . AND LEAP

THE THIRD PRECIOUS INNER STONE and great blessing of walking the Inner Path to True Greatness is Hope. It is a Divinely imbued inspiration that brings peace and security and allows joy and conviction to reside in the Spirit-led heart—no matter the circumstances, no matter the consequences. It goes beyond optimism. It is a powerful, reassuring conviction in the heart of what is Truth—and that Truth and Love are abiding. Hope is difficult to define, yet you do know it when you are lifted by it.

Hope exists beyond ourselves—it comes from a Love from the Divine, which embraces us all, even those who do not acknowledge and feel its presence. And because it is beyond us, we cannot destroy it or diminish it. It is there, it always has been.

What we can do is breathe Hope in and partake of it. And this we do when we allow the Wisdom and Grace of God to enter our hearts.

When Hope fills the heart, the heart begins to realize its destiny—truly, fully. Wisdom awakens the heart and instructs the inner spirit-person. Honor shapes the inner spirit-person with a diligence and discipline that frees the heart and mind to soar—without regret, compromise or doubt. Hope comes like a prayer from God, reminding the heart of its real dreams and passions and whispers: *It's all right. I know. I'm here. We've got work to do.*

Hope sings its song one heart at a time. We can become part of it. We can't create it—it flows from the Divine embrace—but we can glow with it and awaken others to it. Hope is far-sighted. It sees a better tomorrow, even in the midst of chaos, sorrow and pain. It sees the good in the criminal, the reward in a defeated stand for justice, the worth in what is considered lowly, the potential in the arrogant and cruel, the joy in service.

But it is so hard to hold on to Hope when we're bombarded with life. So hard that we give up on it. That's why *we* are not the keepers of it—God is! King David said that he would lift his eyes to the hills of heaven, where, he emphasized, his strength and help came from. He knew that relying on self alone led to folly and failure and that only Wisdom could guide him to success and hope.

"Wait a minute!" you say. "What you're describing is next to impossible for most people to achieve, except for maybe a saint! You're talking about some kind of enlightenment that makes you love everyone, right? I can't do that. Do you really think ordinary people can do that?"

Yep.

Not many have, but all of us can.
I never said it was easy.
I never said it was automatic.
It is a choice.
It requires new skills.

It is a leap of faith in today's culture. But if you leap, you are promised Divine help, guidance, wings—and Hope. If you leap, you are following your heart and your true destiny. If you leap, you will find yourself living incredibly—walking the Inner Path to True Greatness, hand in hand with none other than God.

HOPE AND THE HEARTSKILL OF WISDOM

AND WE COULDN'T ASK for a better traveling partner. By believing and trusting in the Divine, we begin to believe and trust in our own talents, skills and abilities—including the ability to love unconditionally—because we are awakened to the overwhelming Truth that *the Divine believes in us!*

As Wisdom and Truth become the source for our thoughts, the Spirit of God becomes the source for our evolving skills. The skill of Wisdom is honed by the spiritual heart and it sharpens our understanding, our perception and our insight. Many people conceive of great ability, expertise or proficiency in terms of either mental or physical skills. There is a lot more at work than mere mental or physical skills, however, when real results are accomplished.

Let's examine what really happens. Picture Michael Jordan in his red Chicago Bulls uniform, racing down the court. By several steps, he beats a defender to the basket. As Michael nears the basket, Scottie Pippen lobs the ball high in the air. Jordan grabs it in one hand, almost effortlessly dunking it into the net. He lingers there a moment, seemingly suspended in air, before his feet hit the court, propelling him back across the floor.

It is easy to visualize the mental and physical skills of such extraordinary athletes and to imagine the immediate results of their actions on the court. It is more difficult to discern the spiritual and emotional skills that underlie their athletic prowess. When a skilled artist creates a beautiful piece of art, most of us have no difficulty seeing that end result as having originated in the emotions and spirit—or heart—of the artist. More difficult for some is imagining the mental and physical skills possessed by people in the arts and crafts. Often, the end result we attribute to any particular skill—be it athletic, artistic, scientific or of some other variety—is actually the function of a combination of several skills.

Highly skilled individuals use their passion and other heart emotions to energize their other skills—their imagination, thinking and practice—to bring the desired results. Because of this, HeartSkill is the starting point for making the best use of our physical and mental skills, as well as any specialized skills we may have acquired.

THE SPIRITUAL PRINCIPLE OF UNDERSTANDING

WE STARTED LIFE with God-given physical, mental, emotional and spiritual skills or abilities. We each have particular talents and innermost dreams that become more apparent with the infusion of Divine Wisdom and Truth. When we see with wise, honorable, hopeful eyes, we see not only our own potential but the potential impact and good that our abilities and efforts can bring to others. This is exciting stuff!

This realization is the Spirit-induced principle of understanding. It is truly an enlightened state that takes us to a higher level of comprehension of the Divinely inspired knowledge and wisdom we possess. Achieving this state of understanding takes a skilled heart—an open, honest heart that seeks and desires this understanding—and acts upon it. With the honed HeartSkill of Wisdom, we are able to upgrade the original source material in our hearts from mere human wisdom to Divine knowledge and Wisdom. It is this that instructs our hearts toward understanding.

All hearts are skilled to some degree. The level of quality of the skill and to what purpose the heart is predisposed to act differ from person to person. HeartSkill plays a very big part in the development and continued application of all physical, mental, emotional and spiritual skills. The physical and mental skill latent in us would remain dormant or continue to be far less developed in the absence of the heart's emotional and spiritual skills. As with developing any other skill, it takes time to develop these highest skills of the heart.

Wisdom and Truth and its principles are tools for developing highest skills. But only the Spirit of God inside a reborn spirit can make those tools valuable. The principles and values of Wisdom, with the Spirit of God within the reborn spirit, are the only tools that will ensure that our hearts are truly predisposed toward others' interests and not our own. The degree to which we permit Wisdom and the Spirit of God to remain alive in our heart, and allow them to work together to guide and direct our inner life, will determine the level of our HeartSkill.

With God's HeartSkill of Wisdom inside, there is a huge, supernatural enhancement to the human knowledge element, leading to deep heart understanding that does not—and cannot—arise from any other source. This understanding allows you to see through God's eyes, to love and care with a heart full of His inspiration, motive and passion, make choices and take actions based on His higher Wisdom and Honor and true Hope—a solid foundation and certitude that frees the inner spirit-person to follow the Divine path without doubts and with conviction.

The HeartSkill of Wisdom equips us to employ discretion and prudence, two other important spiritual principles. Discretion is the choice to gain the right result through purposeful planning. The first step is to devise ideas and applications of Wisdom's principles of truth. Then we are better equipped to decide preferred courses of action.

Wisdom's discretion and prudence cause us to be cautious and sensible, and ultimately lead us to the most sound and responsible decisions. They produce good judgment in all areas of our lives and create the kind of sound thinking we can use to arrange our life experiences, so that our current emotions, motives and desires will be consistent with Wisdom's motive (unconditional love) and passion (serving God and others before self).

We truly understand when we allow the Spirit of God to live in and work through us. Only then do we possess the HeartSkill of Wisdom that creates in us the MindSet of Wisdom that permits us to see life, ourselves, others and all roles and relationships through the eternal scope of a spiritually wise heart.

HOPE AND PATIENCE

A SKILLED HEART practices patience, is slow to speak, choosing to listen to all sides, leaving room for Hope in all matters. In taking tests and examinations, many of us may have been convinced of the value in deriving and stating the answer quickly. This, combined with our natural instinct to try to prove another wrong, largely explains why we often think too quickly. From a relationship perspective, thinking too quickly is not desirable and often leads to an unwise conclusion and action. The ideal thought process does not involve zooming ahead to beat a stopwatch.

Rather we should think slowly, exploring the surrounding factors and scenarios. We need discretion and prudence, applied skillfully, to be assured of taking wise action. The habit of thinking slowly and using the HeartSkill of Wisdom can greatly enhance our effectiveness as thinkers, and ultimately as doers. Thinking this way helps us concentrate on the Truth, the essentials, at each stage in the decision-making process.

Physical skills, education, human intellect and cleverness cannot make up for deficiencies in heart skills. We all need to possess discretion and prudence and learn how to apply these with skill, so that painful experiences don't teach us hard and often expensive lessons.

The Real Thing

WISDOM AND THE SPIRIT of God, when reborn inside us, empower us with great ability in our hearts to discern what is real and act with prudence. The HeartSkill of Wisdom can bring light and understanding where there has been confusion, division and darkness. The Spirit of God and Wisdom, living within us, greatly enhance the skills we already have. They multiply our talents, sharpen our senses and give us mental alertness, acuity and conscious awareness far beyond our natural faculties. Our heart has spiritual ears that hear with great clarity, spiritual eyes that can perceive the tiniest detail and a MindSet capable of deep understanding of highest thought, knowledge and means. We need to get out of the wishful-thinking MindSet and get into the MindSet of Wisdom, where the spiritually wise heart controls thinking and sees Truth for what it is and is not.

Then we will become beneficiaries of the discretion and prudent wisdom of the heart, leaving folly behind forever. That is the power of Wisdom's HeartSkill.

Judgment of situations, individuals or ourselves is an undertaking too important to be left to the mind. Wise people assign judgment to their wise hearts.

HOPE AND WISDOM'S MOTIVE

You will find, as you look back upon your life, that the moments when you really lived are the moments when you have done things in the spirit of love.

—Henry Drummond

Wisdom's motive is the centerpiece of Eternal Truth and the wellspring of personal and relationship well-being. This is true because well-being springs from the heart. It is in the heart that Wisdom's motive resides. Our dominant motives move us to personal, relationship and leadership choices and actions that result in end consequences. Because of this, the wise person always seeks to base all decisions on Wisdom's motive.

Wisdom's motive is unconditional, God-like love—love for God, others and self. Unconditional love is the guiding dominant motive of people who have the Spirit of God inside. They know that the best love is the love you give. This is love that lets the Spirit of God love through us: It is love based on choice—on an act of will, rather than on feelings or opinions.

The Reverend Dr. Martin Luther King Jr. urges that, as we seek justice, to be sure to move with dignity and discipline, using the weapon of love. He encouraged and inspired us by saying he believed that love is the most durable power in the world.

Dr. King spoke of these things in Montgomery, Alabama, on November 6, 1956, just seven days before the U.S. Supreme Court ruled against Alabama's segregation laws. What was going on in Alabama in 1956 was happening in every other state of the Union as well, in religious and business institutions, not just in government institutions. Sadly, discrimination still continues today in every part of the world, but I believe it can be conquered in time—and time is a but a physical experience. Dr. King's Divinely inspired message of Hope reveals that Truth is on the side of Love.

Wisdom teaches that discrimination against others for any reason is wrong. Happily, there is hope that justice can be achieved when we embrace Wisdom's motive. Justice or injustice is a result of our choices, how we conduct ourselves with one another, every day of our lives. We must stop blaming injustice on institutions. We must realize that the ideal of justice can become reality only through wise individual conduct. We must not just talk about justice, we must do the actions that will create justice. When Wisdom truly rules our hearts, the *agape* (a Greek word that early Christians adopted for God-like unconditional love) of God replaces biases, prejudices and intolerance against others. Wisdom's motive becomes our motive for action. Then we can have unity and understanding. We can blend in harmony, free from conflict. Unconditional love breaks down the walls and levels the playing field. It drives out fear and destroys distrust. Unconditional, selfless love is ego-effacing. It repents and is truly sorrowful about past wrongs. It forgives self, and it humbly and graciously asks others for their forgiveness.

Wisdom's motive focuses on the promise of now. Its focus is today, not the mistakes of the past, the present or the future. It trusts every person and treats them as God does, as unique and precious individuals. Wisdom reaches across the abyss of difference to grasp the hand of likeness, and brings peace that surpasses understanding. Wisdom treats each of us as if eternal destiny depended on its truth. And it does.

We cannot love unconditionally within our human abilities and methodologies. We cannot break ingrained, unwise habits and behaviors. It takes a supernatural, spiritual transplant and transformation to change. Then we must permit our reborn spirit to develop a spiritually wise heart, possessing the Heart-Skill of Wisdom. The Spirit of God must dwell in us, must live and influence through us. It takes true transformation of the inner spirit-person to desire and practice Wisdom's motive and give birth to the graces of compassion, justice and humility.

In his 1964 Nobel Prize acceptance speech, Dr. King declared that unarmed truth and unconditional love will have the final word in reality.

Dr. King's heart knew Hope—and because he chose to believe, value and express that Hope, so many others also discovered Hope.

THE HOPE OF UNCONDITIONAL LOVE

UNCONDITIONAL LOVE is a foreign concept to many people. We all seem to love conditionally by our nature. We love those who love us. We love those who have not wronged us. We love the people we like. We love those whom we decide have earned or deserve our love.

Wisdom's motive is different. It has an indefatigable benevolence, an unconquerable goodwill, which always seeks the highest good of other people, no matter what they do. It does not consider the worthiness of its object. It accepts others as they are and loves them in spite of the circumstances or their behavior. Wisdom's motive is not just a feeling. Unconditional love is not meant simply to make us feel good. It is meant to motivate us, so we will act in ways that emulate God's goodness, in every role and relationship choice and action of our lives. Unconditional love is demanding and sometimes uncomfortable. It may demand that we act in painful, practical, or uncomfortable ways. But we must remember that unconditional love is the responsibility of every individual.

I can never emphasize enough that Wisdom's Motive occurs as an act of the will, not by chance or by pure emotion.

Unconditional love is always truthfully understanding and supportive. Unconditional love listens with attentive ears. Unconditional love is never self-seeking. Therefore, unconditional love will never hurt another person, whether physically or emotionally; will never consider, much less attempt, any deception or manipulation; and will never seek to dominate another person. When unconditional love seeks change, it is gentle and kind, and approaches another person humbly and graciously. Saint Paul said unconditional love is patient and kind, never jealous or envious, never boastful or proud. Love is never haughty, selfish or rude. Love does not demand its way. It is not irritable or touchy. It does not hold grudges or notice when others do something incorrectly. Unconditional love is never glad at injustice, but rejoices when Truth wins out. Saint Paul said that if we love someone unconditionally we will continue to love that person, no matter what the cost. Wisdom's motive bears specific and obvious fruit and it cannot be faked. Therein lies the power of Wisdom's motive.

HOPE AND WISDOM'S PASSION

THOSE THINGS WE VALUE most become the passions of our life. We can fool a lot of people about the truth of our treasures, but it is impossible to fool our hearts. Our treasures—our passions—live in our hearts, and thus are inseparable from them. Whatever we treasure most in life is what we will most certainly throw our total being into.

I have found that material possessions, status and wealth cannot compare to what people and relationships mean. Possessions and status never brought me or anyone else the true happiness, satisfaction and joy for which we each deeply long. I found those only when I made the personal choice to treasure my personal, harmonious spiritual relationship with God. The inner spiritual peace from that relationship ignited in me the passion for relationships with my children, family, friends and associates.

Wise individuals nurture those passions in their personal and work lives. The number one priority of our everyday living and working should be that our outer actions be guided by Wisdom's inner personal character and integrity. This will ensure that enduring purpose becomes and remains the first priority of our lives.

Wisdom's inner character and integrity have two key components:

1. a spiritually wise heart (HeartSkill of Wisdom)
2. a servant's attitude (MindSet of Wisdom).

The heartbeat and the habitual MindSet of all should be true caregiving. To serve others first requires a pure heart as the guide. Wisely serving others requires a spiritually wise heart. Guidance and direction from a spiritually wise heart move us to respect one another so much that our priority and passion will be satisfaction of others.

Wisdom's selfless, gracious-servant principle teaches that those who desire to be served must first serve. Wisdom's passion leads us always to put ourselves in the other person's position, to ask, "What does this person need?" and then to work to ensure that the need is fulfilled.

Wisdom's passion is true servantlike humility. When we serve, we should be humble, pleasant and gracious. Our servantlike humility should be easily detected by those served, but never paraded in an attempt to win praise for our efforts.

CHANGING YOUR MINDSET: TREASURE HUNTING FOR HOPE

There is no medicine like hope, no incentive so great, no tonic so powerful as expectation of something tomorrow.
—O. S. Marden

The late Dr. Norman Vincent Peale reminded us that, "We tend to get what we expect." Our life shapes itself in response to our outlook from our outpost inside. The outpost inside is where the queen or king really lives and where all the really important stuff goes on. The creative power within us can either bring us to abundance or drive us to destruction.

We should not be afraid to go out on a limb, because out on that limb is where the fruit hangs. But before we place our hopes in a philosophy of living and working, we want to make sure that philosophy's soil is enduring, that it will grow trees that produce the truly satisfying fruit we are hoping will be there when we go out on that limb.

One of the best things we can do in our lives is to begin again in Hope. The beginning point is inside each of us. Wisdom is the first and most important inner ingredient. With Wisdom inside, we possess the HeartSkill and MindSet of Wisdom with their three inner qualities of Wisdom, Honor and Hope. These enduring qualities mark the Inner Path to True Greatness. They equip, empower and motivate each of us to be a successful human being. That's what really counts.

PROTESTERS WELCOME

SOME SO-CALLED REALIST might protest:

"Come on, Cecil, there is no absolute right and wrong. Anything goes. as long as I don't think it hurts me or others. Hope is just hokum. I'm too busy making money to waste my time on a servant philosophy. You must be kidding about being sublime and leaving footprints on the sands of time. Have you been doing business on Pluto or Mars for the past twenty years? Hey, you've got some nice thoughts and theories, but they'll never work in the real world. Or at least not as well as the means I currently employ to enrich my wallet. Okay, so sometimes someone gets hurt in the process of making myself and my employer a little wealthier. That's not my fault. I'm just doing what's best for me. It's inevitable that someone will get caught in the crossfire. That's what the real business world is like. Thanks for the advice, Cecil, but your Philosophy of Wisdom and MindSet of Wisdom just won't cut it in the dog-eat-dog real world. Close the door on your way out. I gotta take a call."

To this so-called realist I answer:

"I understand. I've been there. Done that. I've been the guy who says, It's okay. Look the other way. It's okay. Nobody gets hurt. It's okay to bend 'em and twist 'em. I know all about trying to achieve so-called greatness through my own business prowess and my self-serving drive and greed."

Some learn, as I did, that possessions and the overwhelming

need for possessions do not fill the void—they deepen the void! Some learn that being filled starts by recognizing the inner spirit-person, which comes from God to dwell in our physical body. Some never learn or, like me, learn only after the costs of the lessons have become very, very substantial in spiritual, emotional and financial terms.

Those who seek the inner spiritual path home to our Creator God know that enduring relationships based on truly important purpose will satisfy that need.

When we compromise or exclude Wisdom's values from our roles and relationships, we prostitute ourselves, exchanging our eternal values for transient pleasures. The nature of this exchange is frightening: ours and others' inner well-being for money, possessions, power, status and esteem.

FEAR

CONSIDER THE FOLLOWING, especially if you have concerns about switching to the inner spiritual path of Wisdom, Honor and Hope: *Running away from fear strengthens its hold over you and extends its power.* And make no mistake, it is fear that makes you scoff at enlightenment. Fear. After all, you would have to change, wouldn't you? In fact, you would have to change how you see yourself—you would have to look inward—deeply inward to the spiritual connection you've denied. And your affluence is at stake—maybe. If you changed, how could you maintain your competitive edge? Your drive? How could you maintain your lifestyle?

Fear. Fear. Fear.

Recognize it for what it is and then—in a quiet, reflective moment—admit that there was once, and still is, a part of you that yearns to be assigned a noble task. A noble mission that gives your life meaning and significance. A relevant, important cause that is so custom-made for you that you find it almost easy to rethink your priorities and values. A noble task that requires your specific talents and personality. And, incredibly, you have secretly always dreamed of doing exactly what this noble task demands of you.

It exists. And the rest of us need you to believe this. But it will entail choice and change, turning from fear and turning inward.

My dad used to say that smart people learn from their mistakes, while wise ones learn from others' mistakes. We all learn the consequences of our choices, sooner or later. But not all learn the lessons of those consequences. Learning and changing have brought the best results into my life.

For your sake and the sake of everyone you love and influence, if you are on the road of folly, stop and retrace your steps to the fork in the road where you took the wrong turn. Fear not. Turn onto the path to Wisdom, Honor and Hope and begin your journey anew in the direction of excellence and lasting success!

THE BUSINESS OF LIFE IS LIVING, NOT BUSINESS

OUR SOCIETY MAY seem to tell us that people want riches. Wisdom shows us that what people *need* fulfillment. True prosperity lies within us, in our hearts and minds. People matter most. And people care how much we care far more than how much we know, how much we have or how we use what we know to earn the income to buy what we have.

We are truly successful when we possess for ourselves—and help others achieve for themselves—total mental, emotional and spiritual well-being. We need to return to Wisdom's beliefs, principles and values, personally and in the professional world if we expect individual and professional distinction. Educated know-how, technology and compromise, unmediated by a spiritually wise heart, have led us down the primrose path where value and priority are placed on material possessions and social status, rather than on true character and integrity, others' well-being and harmonious and unbroken relationships.

THERE IS REAL HOPE

THOMAS CARLYLE the Scottish philosopher, wrote, "Out of the lowest depths there is a path to the loftiest height." These words came to life for me over the past sixteen years, as I climbed out of a deep hole and found the inspiration and the source of strength that permitted me to go from the lowest depths to the loftiest heights.

From whom or where does your strength come? I am asking about your spiritual strength rather than your physical strength. Your inner spiritual strength can fortify your emotions and see you through the most difficult of times. Your inner spiritual strength will lead you to find Hope in what may seem to be a hopeless situation. We are not promised life without sorrow, pain or hardship. In difficult times we can grow the most, if we have at the foundation and center of our life a harmonious, personal spiritual relationship with God. Then we will have at our disposal God's Wisdom, Honor and Hope. God's knowledge, ethic and inspiration are more powerful than ours. With the Spirit of God inside us, our inner spiritual strength is magnified many times over, being supernatural in origin and effect!

Philosophies of folly fail their loyal followers sooner or later. Some work for only a few days, others last longer, but all fail in the end. These philosophies have flawed foundations. They may sound good but they are deadly because they are founded on self as god and on principles and values without Truth. Truth is what is. It is the highest reality, whether we understand or not. Often Truth is the supernatural, not yet naturally understood.

Many live life somewhere between the place where things have gone to hell in a handbasket and the place where things are looking pretty good, at least for the moment. Too often, they succumb to fear and lose hope. Wise people, those who have embraced the Philosophy of Wisdom, have a higher source of inspiration, knowledge, ethics and power from which to draw.

When you are faced with the death of a loved one, financial disaster or health problems, where do you turn? Do you get angry and make your life "hell on earth"? Do you just ignore the situation, hoping it will go away? Or do you have that special and personal, spiritual relationship that allows you to dip into God's vast reservoir and receive strength beyond measure? I am talking about a personal, one-on-one, spiritual relationship directly with the Divine Source of our strength. Through that intimate, personal, spiritual relationship, God can give you the strength you need to face any situation.

God can be our refuge and fortress, if we let Him. God can give us access to the strength, the comfort and the "peace that passeth all understanding."

HOPE IS A HEARTFELT CHOICE

DIVINE ENLIGHTENMENT can help us understand events that may seem totally senseless and completely unfair. Why do bad things sometimes happen to good people? Where was God when the bad thing happened? Doesn't the Divine care?

Let's answer the last two questions first. The Divine is always present with us in spirit. And yes, God cares so much that you and I, members of the greatest Divine creation, were given the freedom of choice and God's unconditional love.

Now let's answer the first question. I believe the answer lies in the God-given freedom of choice we all have. Because each of us has that liberty, good people can be terribly affected by others' unwise choices. If freedom of choice were taken from us, we would be right to point fingers skyward. But none of us wants our freedoms taken away, especially the freedom to choose.

Ann Landers says we should "expect trouble as an inevitable part of life, and when it comes, hold your head high, look it squarely in the eye, and say, 'I will be bigger than you.' " If life's tragedies have left you confused, angry, badly bruised and disappointed, summon every ounce of your resolve and commit yourself to stand tall and follow through on even the smallest tasks every day. Do it, even if it feels unnatural right now. And be encouraged, knowing that, in time, the Divine mends broken hearts, dreams, lives, relationships, and families.

God helps us see that to grow we must heal, and to heal we must let go.

Choose to believe in Divine Hope, let go of the past and leave the desert of "why," knowing that farther along you will understand. You will, you can, you must!

FROM DOUBTS TO STRENGTHS AND BLESSINGS

DOUBTS LIVE BEHIND the heart's door, hidden inside little boxes we build. Allowed to stay there, fears or doubt pop open the boxes, jump up and down, make scary faces and freeze us in our tracks, keeping us from moving forward.

Doubts in the storms of life are normal. Though they bring current discomfort and inner conflict, doubts can lead us to what I call the "intellectual spiritual search," which presents wonderful opportunities for wise change. These opportunities arise from knowing and understanding ourselves, our creator and others better. Faith and Hope are the heart's eyes and higher intellect, the spiritual vision and knowledge that drive fear from our spirit as we soar beyond doubt.

The storms of life often disguise the strengths we will discover from them and the blessings their lessons will lead us to in the future. Consider your past successes and all you went through to attain them. Each was a learning experience that made you who you are today.

Though it may well take time before you understand today's difficulties, you can grow from them as you move hopefully into a brighter, better future. The storms of life are opportunities to pause, to reconnect to God, yourself and others, to learn and grow from adversity, to discover strengths and future blessings in today's difficulties.

THE POWER OF HOPE

BELIEF AND HOPE are key to healing, recovery, renewal and future achievement. A trusting heart is a believing heart, one at peace, full of hope. This serene scene has no place for anxiety, fear or worry. An old French proverb expresses this thought well: "By believing in roses, one brings them to bloom." Picture the beauty of roses in faith. Wisdom plants them, Honor waters them, Hope believes that they will be beautiful and fragrant.

A heart full of hope is guided by wise ambition and is brimming with confidence, continually moving its owner in the direction of true success. Emily Dickinson described a believing, hopeful heart when she penned:

Hope is the thing with feathers—
That perches in the soul—
And sings the tune without the words—
And never stops—at all.

Believe and put to work the power of Wisdom that gets us through the difficulties of today and tomorrow and sustains our hope of a brighter and blessed future.

A REFUGE IN HOPE AND PRAYER

IN THE MIDST OF CHANGE, difficulties or success, taking refuge in Divine Hope, we can rest, find peace and discover new strengths. Refreshment and new strength are found in the sanctuary of Divine refuge.

Alone time with the Divine, in the special and private inner room of our soul, brings everything into proper perspective. The Prophet Isaiah said that God's thoughts and ways are higher than ours, as far as heaven is above earth.

Strength and power are found in inner calmness and peace. Those are best attained in prayer and meditation, supreme opportunities for direct connection to the Divine. In prayer and meditation, we connect directly to the Divine's thoughts and ways.

REJOICE AND BE GLAD

REJOICING AND GLADNESS nurture the soul, rekindling its Hope. Regardless of our circumstances, we are wise to count our blessings and to rejoice and be glad, knowing that our blessings far outweigh life's hardships.

By rejoicing and being glad, we invite laughter, tears of joy, peace and immeasurable hope for a brighter, better future.

SOLVING PROBLEMS

WELCOME DIFFICULTIES and problems. They are opportunities. Their challenges are the launching pad to the level of thinking required to get through hard times and fix problems. Albert Einstein had this process in mind when he said that you cannot solve problems with the same level of thinking that created them.

With Wisdom as our guide, we become a higher inner being, one who thinks on the next level. That higher plane of thinking leads us to live honorably and to have wise and hopeful attitudes and most sound judgment.

When the seeds of truth are picked up and planted in better soil, they are the seeds of permanent, hopeful and wise solutions to our problems. Following the inner path of Truth in our decision making assures us of getting past difficulties, fixing problems, and fulfilling our life's highest potential.

HEART, WHERE THE HOME IS

TRUE GREATNESS SPRINGS from a wise, honorable and hopeful heart. HeartSmarts are life's most important lessons learned and retained in the heart, as the guide for the future. At the center of our soul, HeartSmarts are an ever-flowing fountain of knowledge, ethic and inspiration that have the HeartSkill of Wisdom that leads to a life of true greatness. The way we are inside counts the most. When our hearts are inspired by the Divine, our lives will mirror God's knowledge, beauty, honor, majesty and power. With the inner sunshine of Truth in our hearts, we keep our highest aspirations always in view and wisely move toward them each day. We pursue our higher purpose.

CELEBRATING LIFE

DANCE ON THE CLOUDS, gleefully rejoice, sing and make music, celebrate life! Human life, what a wonderful and hopeful gift! Celebrate it. Praise the Giver.

Have a grand adventure! Maybe you'll get a little wet or hurt, maybe you won't be safe from life's slings and arrows, but you will be truly living. By living every moment as though special, we enjoy it today and tomorrow, and we store up benefits in eternity. Life is a gift. What we do with it is our gift back to the Giver of life.

MY FATHER'S PASSION

MY FATHER WAS THE BEST LEADER, mentor and role example I have ever known. Many of his qualities will probably strike some people as unorthodox. He sought peace with all, making friends rather than enemies by being kind, friendly and respectful to all. My father was thankful and grateful and felt blessed just for having a job in the local factory. He knew that gratitude was the heart's memory.

My father respected his employer, his friends, his family and even his enemies. His character was manifested quietly every day with integrity. He let his conduct do his talking.

My father always gave and shared more than what was expected or required of him. Whether the gift was of his time, his skill, his influence or his money, my dad was generous. Without fanfare he used his time, skill, influence, money and material possessions to do kind things for those who could not do for themselves. He was unselfish, not driven by greed or desire to gain for himself; he was not a taker.

His passion was Wisdom's passion—serving others and being a blessing to them by sharing with them.

My father taught me the importance of purpose, clear vision and commitment to mission. More than anything else, he taught me the honor of serving and caregiving for others' interests ahead of self-interests. He modeled for me the power of Wisdom's passion. And because he maintained a spirit of Hope, I and many others have been enriched and blessed.

NUGGET OF INSPIRATION

It is from numberless diverse acts of courage and belief that human history is shaped. Each time a man stands up for an ideal, or acts to improve the lot of others, or strikes out against injustice, he sends forth a tiny ripple of hope.
—Robert F. Kennedy

CHAPTER EIGHT

SPIRITUAL TRANSFORMATION

Lives of great men all remind us
We can make our lives sublime,.
And, departing, leave behind us
Footprints on the sands of time.
                    —Henry Wadsworth Longfellow

Let me tell you what it took to finally cause me to embrace Wisdom's principles, its motive and passion priorities in every compartment and corner of my personal and business life. This story demonstrates more vividly than anything else I've said so far—that our life is like a currency that can be spent only once. When I learned this lesson, I decided to spend the remaining currency of my life on Wisdom's priorities: Wisdom's motive and passion. Certainly I still fall short every day, but Wisdom inside keeps picking me back up and even carrying me sometimes.

DEATHBED LESSON

IT WAS NOT QUITE 5:00 A.M. on a Monday when our home telephone rang. I listened as my mother cried softly on the other end, sharing with me her certainty that her beloved husband of almost fifty years had died while she was visiting him in intensive care around 4:30 A.M. Later she called back to confirm that he had passed away.

I attempted to console my mother in both conversations, telling her that I loved her very much and would be there soon. Yet I admit to you, I was completely stunned. I listened in silence, for the most part.

Several weeks earlier, a sense of urgency had suddenly gripped me inside. I privately considered what I'd felt to be the unspoken, soft voice of God, clearly telling me that my father's journey here on earth would soon be over. (God has never spoken to me audibly, but has graced me with an unspoken message from time to time.) The possibility of his impending death was difficult for me to believe. My father had always been, as we say in the country, as healthy as a horse.

Yet a few days after that unspoken message, Dad's health quickly spiraled downward. Quadruple bypass surgery was scheduled.

I had seen pain in his eyes when I visited him in recovery. As I held my father's hand that day, prayed with him and kissed his brow, affirming my love, he squeezed my hand to acknowledge that he was quite ready to meet God. I thanked God that day for my father, and for letting me know what the probable outcome of his surgery would be.

Mere weeks later, here was my mother calling me to say that my father was dead. After I hung up the telephone, I cried softly as a tidal wave of emotion swept over me, leaving an emptiness that I cannot describe. The emotions momentarily controlled every fiber of my inner being and of my outer physical body. They left a void that lasted for some time.

There were two reasons I was so stunned by my father's death. First, no one in our immediate family had died before, so this was a totally new experience. Since my father's death, I have talked with many who have lost close loved ones. It seems that the more immediate the relationship, the more devastating the loss and the greater the grief. Just from observing my mother, I could see how much harder the loss of my father was on her than it was on me and my siblings.

Second, my father was the greatest man and the greatest

leader I have ever known. No one else even comes close. I say this despite his faults and weaknesses—which he battled and learned from. Even though my wife, Patty, and I moved away from our childhood homes more than twenty-five years before my father's death, my respect for Big C never diminished. My admiration for him only grew as the years passed—in spite of those inevitable selfish moments, when I wished my father had been different in a few areas. As I matured, I understood much better how he had sacrificed, how loving he had been and what a marvelous leadership example he had set for me. He was truly an outstanding man and leader, but more than that, he was an outstanding father.

My father's wise heart and servant MindSet guided him in every role he played in life. He had the MindSet and HeartSkill of Wisdom and practiced its caregiving strategy as husband, father, employee, supervisor and leader on the job, as a friend to so many. The words in an old hymnal say that my father and I will meet again on that beautiful shore, in that land far beyond forever, in the sweet by-and-by. God has healed my heart and mind over the years, and now I have a healed perspective about my father's death.

God's intended lesson to me and others has not gone unnoticed. Though the pain, heartache and longing to see and talk to my dad remain, the void is gone. God has filled it with Divine Presence in my inner being. As promised on the pages of Wisdom, God has used my father's death for my good and for the good of many others. Career success, money, power, possessions, status or others' esteem cannot compare to my beautiful memories of my dad or the wisdom I learned from him.

DANCE, DON'T SIT OUT LIFE

WE CAN HAVE one of three responses to tragedy and crisis. In these and in other life-defining times:
1. We can become emotionally and spiritually numb from denial.
2. We can allow them to destroy us and affect others we influence.

3. We can use them as seeds for growth and greater success in our lives.

We all fear loss. Loss of love, relationships, companionship, fellowship, money, health, comfort, esteem, respect, control, choice and on and on. As my writing friend Carl DeVilbiss says, loss is a natural part of life. Carl told me, "Cecil, we lose our baby teeth, our childhood, our parents, our immaturity, our perfect eyesight and some—like you and me—lose our hair!"

We can choose to view loss as an opportunity to heal and grow. To grow, we must heal, and to heal, we must let go. We cannot stand still when we incur losses, because eventually we will go backward into an abyss. To heal and grow, we must grieve our losses, honor them in the very personal way that we alone know is the right way for each of us. To deny feelings of pain, to shove them down and refuse their validity, engenders other really destructive feelings such as rage, hostility and depression. Happily, God provides us with the ability to make wise choices. We can learn to express our grief and our pain, to see the Hope in our losses and wisely move toward that Hope. Then we can release our losses. Healing comes when we find in our pain and tears the seeds of growth and Hope.

GIVE FAITH A FIGHTING CHANCE

NONE OF US IS PROMISED tomorrow, and eventually we all make that step into eternity. In the wise words of Charles E. Hummel, "We realize our dilemma goes deeper than shortage of time; it is basically a problem of priorities . . . We confess . . . we have left undone those things we ought to have done; and we have done those things which we ought not to have done."

One of the best things we can do in our lives is to begin again. And the beginning point is inside. Yesterday is gone, and tomorrow may or may not come. Today will become whatever we make of it.

Life can be a beautiful journey when through faith we individually accept God's redemptive plan for humanity. We must open our hearts to allow the Spirit of God to come in, live there and provide Divine inspiration and guidance so that we can live by enduring principles and values. We must put aside the quest for an image that will impress others. We each can be the person we are meant to be. And when we become that person, then our dreams really do come true.

If you are yearning for a deeper spiritual and emotional connection and searching for the standard and principles of truth for running your life, then the connective power and reassurance of Divine Truth is your answer. If you are searching for meaning and can't find it in bigger paychecks and lofty promotions, then Wisdom is your point of connection. If you need an antidote to rampant and excessive ambition, cutthroat competition and greed for greed's sake, Wisdom, Honor and Hope are your answers.

If you are looking for true significance, satisfaction, security and sanity, then put Wisdom at the center of your life.

SAY GOOD-BYE TO HUMANISM AND MAN-MADE RELIGION

WHEN TRANSFORMATION OCCURS inside us, we are given a new spirit, complete with a new heart and mind. Each of us can have a personal spiritual relationship with God. Living with Wisdom, Honor and Hope is a manner of inner spiritual being and lifestyle that results from a personal spiritual relationship with God.

Practicing religious rituals and living and working by humanly inspired rules and regulations does not create the vital inner spirituality I am teaching. Outward behavior changes only when the first priority of our living and working is inner spirituality, Wisdom's way. Then, through the inspiration and power of the Spirit of God living in us and influencing us to live Wisdom, we experience real and enduring success and significance.

What happens next is the process of inversion inside us. Inversion means the reversal of a normal position, order or relationship. Inversion occurs when we embrace and apply the idea that we should make spirituality a priority. As Jesus taught, we should seek first the kingdom of God and God's righteousness, then all other things will be added. Inversion means we alter or reverse our relative values. Old values are turned upside down.

The spiritual principles of transformation and inversion must be effected in our inner spiritual lives if we are ever to possess the MindSet of Wisdom. When these are effected, the process of possessing a spiritually wise heart and servant attitude begins. These are absolutely essential inner traits for attaining truly lasting success in personal and business roles and relationships.

A FACELIFT WON'T DO

HANDLING OUR CHOICES and actions wisely is not a matter of saying "I will," and controlling our thoughts. We must go deeper. We must change the internal inspirational "database" from which our thoughts are developed. That demands that we change our internal operating system to Wisdom.

Of course, we can choose to think, reason and act according to our own cleverness. We can continue to use our existing database. This would not be a wise choice, since this manner of thinking may have created role and relationship problems before. The better choice is to appropriate Wisdom and Truth and its principles and values as the basis for our thought processes. Then we can alter our thinking by changing the heart source of our thinking material.

Some people believe thinking is similar to walking and breathing. They feel there is nothing we can do or really need to do about our thinking. They merely accept their present level of thinking and neither desire improvement, nor perceive the need for it.

Wisdom, however, teaches us that when the database of raw material changes, our thoughts change. When our thoughts change, our actions change. Wise people know that thinking is a skill that can be enhanced greatly by improving the quality of thinking material and developing higher quality decision models through habitually thinking and acting upon highest, heart-held inspiration and know-how.

Wisdom is the highest heart-held inspiration and know-how, and the HeartSkill of Wisdom is deep-heart understanding of how to best apply Wisdom.

We can all learn to be better thinkers, and the best way to improve our thinking is Divinely inspired Wisdom and Truth inside as our source material of thinking. Through the influence of the Spirit of God, we can develop the HeartSkill of Wisdom to apply wise and meaningful goals, principles, and values to our lives in the best possible ways. These are the heart tools and empowerment mechanisms to make our hearts the most highly skilled instrument. While we may reason in our minds, Wisdom teaches us that we are as we think in our hearts.

The desire to learn is important. Equally important are the faith and courage to apply what we learn. Each of us has the God-given capacity and skill to acquire a reasonable amount of thinking skill and, with Wisdom inside, we possess the highest thinking know-how and skill. We all can increase our thinking skill, regardless of our IQ, when Wisdom and Truth undergird the process. As with other skills, such as skiing, the more we practice thinking, the better it gets. When skiers' practice only on the bunny slopes, they never acquire the skills they need to keep the blue and black trails from turning them black and blue! But with Wisdom as our trail guide, we can improve our thinking skills so dramatically that we can master any expert trail with the calm assurance of an Olympic skier. The secret is learning to think and make choices with a heart full of Wisdom and Truth, guided by the Spirit of God.

LIVING TO THE BEAT OF A DIFFERENT DRUMMER

IT IS NOT POSSIBLE to live the life I am talking about, unless purity of personal spirituality is achieved through a choice of personal faith in the biblical plan of redemption. That done, each person must choose to allow the Spirit of God to come and live in their spirit, transform their heart and mind and reverse his other priorities to those of Wisdom.

These are your beginning points. Any attempt to pursue a course of personal, leadership, relationship or on-the-job conduct consistent with Wisdom will yield less than your very best or may end in disaster, unless you first trust in the God of Wisdom. Trust in what the God of Wisdom has already done, and change your priorities to those of Wisdom.

The Philosophy of Wisdom and its tools cannot be understood, possessed or applied by the natural heart. It takes a new spirit, complete with a new heart and mind. The learning process continues over time. Psychologists indicate that we cannot stop an unwise habit by simply resolving to stop it and then stopping it. We can stop an unwise habit only by first mentally, emotionally and spiritually resolving to do so, *then* mentally, emotionally and spiritually developing a wise habit to replace the unwise habit. In practice, actually ending an unwise habit requires replacing it simultaneously with a wise habit. Changing bad habits and destructive behavior requires modification of thinking and behavior.

There are two types of changing one's thinking and behavior: (1) the type that comes about because of human self-discipline, and (2) the better, more productive, internalized form that comes about because the inner spirit-person adopts Wisdom and its principles and values as the guide for thinking, decision making, and actions.

The inner spirit-person must be remade to effect real, long-term, durable, wise habits in exchange for current unwise role and relationship habits. It is not enough to seek self-control through the application of self-discipline to outward behavior, because the inner spirit-person controls the choices that are manifest in the outer person. To achieve highest excellence and enduring success in our personal and business roles and relationships, we must take action to change our hearts, if they are not currently guided by Wisdom. Our hearts will then educate and retrain our minds.

Paradigms in our hearts, minds and lives can be shifted by such methods as learning from mistakes, from accidents or from insight and wisdom. I recommend embracing Wisdom, the inspiration of Wisdom, and allowing the Spirit of God permanently inside the inner room of the soul. This is, by far, the best way to effect truly valuable change in our hearts, minds and lives. Significant, important change comes from the inside out, not the outside in. We cannot escape our accountability for the impact and influence on others of our choices in roles and relationships. We are responsible. If Albert Einstein was correct when he asserted that working within existing ways of thinking will not produce any new models—and I believe he was correct in that assertion—then we must change the way we think. The Philosophy of Wisdom offers practices, procedures and ideas to follow that will help each of us to reach and maintain the highest excellence in our thinking and actions, and to gain enduring benefits for ourselves and everyone with whom we come in contact.

FIRST THINGS FIRST

THERE CAN BE ONLY ONE highest priority in our lives. When that priority is inner peace—Wisdom's way, the way of the Bible— we become more able to resist the outside pressures of our materialistic and hedonistic society and to stay on the Inner Path to True Greatness. Inner peace is a prerequisite to developing the HeartSkill and MindSet of Wisdom that assure you of achieving true greatness.

REACH FOR THE STARS

The fourth dimension is the spiritual realm. Dreams and visions are the language of the fourth dimension. The Spirit of God speaks through visions and dreams.
—Dr. David Yonggi Cho

THE INITIAL TOOL for possessing anything is seeing it, envisioning yourself in possession. The Divine Spirit working in and through you can develop the HeartSkill and MindSet of Wisdom, with their higher vision and power to work in the spiritual and physical realms to cause higher inner vision and dreams to become reality.

When you possess the HeartSkill of Wisdom you will have the faith and courage to visualize goals as completed, before ever beginning the process of achieving them. Personal faith in God gives you higher vision and wisest perspective; the Spirit of God within you will ensure that your heart holds wise desires. Then, in the imagination, you will see through the eternal scope of a spiritually wise heart that envisions things that are not yet as though they already are. Through the spiritual principles of choice, concentration and habit, you can keep on seeing those pictures in your heart's eye, until your partnership with God brings them into reality.

Wise desires that are the foundation of the HeartSkill and MindSet of Wisdom are yours through spiritual transformation, which takes place when you allow the Spirit of God to come and live in perfect union with your human spirit. Then you will experience a new, higher level of inner vision and thinking based on Eternal Truth and on the inversion of your values and priorities to the eternally important ones. You will have the highest moral compass, God's Honor, within you and the courage to do the right thing for the right reason. Your faith will be faith that is lived for higher purpose, not flaunted for show.

When you develop the HeartSkill and MindSet of Wisdom, you see better inwardly, think wisely, make wise choices and speak positively. You become truly patient, always waiting on God's timing rather than pushing to make things happen. You no longer strive in your own power and methods to bring about your visions and dreams. Instead you rest in the Lord, as you allow the Spirit of God to work in and through your human spirit.

God-imparted faith inspires Divine imagination, thoughts, words and actions. These are the greatest creative tools in the physical or spiritual realms. The Spirit of God living in your inner spirit-person Divinely works through your faith, imagination, thoughts, words and actions. Rest assured, what is hatched in the heart of your inner spirit-person and spoken aloud will become your MindSet and play out in your circumstances.

So if you want improved circumstances in the physical realm or desire a radical change in the spiritual or physical realm, first you must see better inside and speak and act according to that better vision. The solution begins by allowing the Spirit of God to live in your human spirit. It becomes reality as your Spirit-controlled heart imparts Divine desires and faith that fuel you to dream big dreams, have higher vision and thought, speak and act in ways that bring the inner spirit-person's dreams and visions into existence. So, as the Bible says, it is not by human might or power, but by the Spirit of God working within and through you.

If God lives within you, you have the foundation for life that will not shift. From it, you will develop the HeartSkill of Wisdom and thus possess highest sight and the resources to change your MindSet to the MindSet of Wisdom. This vision and power is the Spirit of God loving, working, creating and changing through you and your boldness. This is the Perfect Union: the Divine Spirit linked to your human spirit, connected at the heart of your soul.

When you travel the Inner Path to True Greatness, you don't travel alone. You travel with all other enlightened souls who chose to live fully—both spiritually and physically. Because you also travel with the Divine Spirit, you will walk with a loving, awesome power that opens your heart and mind to a better way of living, serving and working.

Allowed by a personal choice of faith to live in the innermost room of your soul, the Spirit of God gives you the three precious inner stones I also refer to as the inner spiritual lenses of Wisdom, Honor and Hope. Together they create in you the Heart-Skill and MindSet of Wisdom that equips you with spiritual vision, power and skill to recognize and rise above narrow dreams and folly.

NUGGET OF INSPIRATION

Unless one is born anew, he or she cannot enter the kingdom of God . . .That which is born of the flesh is flesh, and that which is born of the Spirit is spirit . . . the Divine Spirit gives new life, eternal life.

—(personal paraphrase of) Jesus

God loved the world so much, he gave his only Son so that anyone who believes in Him shall have eternal life.

—(personal paraphrase of the gospel of) John

CHAPTER NINE

FIVE HABITS OF TRUE GREATNESS

We become what our most dominant thoughts are.
—Earl Nightingale

INNER PROGRAMMING WITH WISDOM AND ETERNAL TRUTH

THE DOMINANT THOUGHTS of our hearts are the origin of all our habits. These heart thoughts build and nurture our character. As the mind adopts these heart thoughts, they become plans and choices, and, eventually, actions—repeated over and over again, until they become habits.

The habits of true greatness have a heart filled with Wisdom and Eternal Truth as their wellspring. As the Spirit of God directs our hearts, our characters are remolded. Our plans and choices become pure. Our actions—repeated over and over again—serve God's will. There are, of course, many more than five habits one develops when one lives by Wisdom and Eternal Truth inside. In this chapter I share the five that have been most meaningful to me.

HABIT 1
THINK WISDOM'S THOUGHTS AND
FOLLOW WISDOM'S WAYS

READ AT LEAST ONE chapter a day from Scripture. Spend time meditating on what you read. Then, with the Spirit of God's help, live out in your daily conduct what you learned from the reading and meditation.

Program yourself to use Wisdom's thinking system and make your decisions in Wisdom's way. Wisdom instructs us that God's thoughts and ways are as much above ours, as the heavens are above the earth. If we want the best results, we must have and rely on the highest source of heart-held inspiration, thought and skill. Saint Paul taught that we are to have Wisdom as our food source for thought.

HABIT 2
PRAY

TO KNOW THE WAY UP and down the mountain, ask the One who made the mountain.

Prayer is an invisible tool that can make a very visible difference. Pray about everything, small or great. Stay in a prayerful attitude all the time. Develop the habit of listening, not just talking. Try forgetting any preestablished agenda you have, and consider praying this way: "God, show me clearly what are the wise choices and actions for me to take to ensure that other people's interests are best served."

And be sure, when you pray, to always, always first thank God for life's blessings. Take time to thank the Divine for specific blessings like health and family and answers to specific past prayers.

I like to start and end my day in time alone with God, studying Wisdom's pages, worshiping God and praying. It's amazing how much better my attitude becomes when I do that.

The Life-changing Power of Prayer Is Real
CONSIDER TWO STORIES from a prayer warrior, my wife, Patty.

What's faster than a speeding bullet and can leap tall

buildings in a single bound? SUPERMAN! Everyone loves him because he does the impossible and always shows up just in time to save the day! Superman, however, does have one flaw—he's fictional.

There is someone faster than a speeding bullet who jumps tall buildings in a single bound. He is supernatural—but He is real and really does come on the scene when He is called upon! I know this from many experiences.

When our daughter, Heather, was in the fourth grade she became very sick with Rocky Mountain Spotted Fever. Her temperature remained at a frightening 105 degrees for several days, regardless of what I attempted.

I awoke at three o'clock one morning feeling an urgency to pray for her. Her temperature was still 105, so I placed my hands upon her body and prayed for a miracle. Fifteen minutes later I took her temperature again. It had dropped to 102 degrees! I knew that God heard and answered my prayer. Medicine and science affirmed my faith when a blood test fifteen years later proved Heather not only had RMSF, but antibodies still in her bloodstream revealed that she had survived a normally lethal case. God had truly been our "Superman," showing up just in time to save the day!

—Patty Kemp

My Grandmother Robertson had a powerful influence on me and countless others, though she never traveled more than a few miles from her rural Mississippi farm. She appeared a simple, even ordinary person by society's standards, yet she made this world a better place to live.

Three times a day, she would slip away to a special place outside the house to be alone with God. There she would read the Bible, meditate, reflect and tell God of her own needs as well as others. Those times were her priority. And because of that dedication, she influenced lives and watched them change.

She would briefly escape the clamor of raising eleven children, cooking meals, cleaning house and dozens of other responsibilities. Sometimes I try to use my busy schedule to

justify not spending time alone with God. When I do, I am re-
minded of how Grandmother Robertson didn't. Her example
is frozen in my memory, reminding me to never get too busy
to neglect my alone time—and reflection—with God—
which brings everything into proper perspective.

Now I understand the value of something Grandmother
Robertson often said, paraphrasing Saint Paul: With prayer
and thanksgiving make your requests known to God and
the peace of God will come on wings from heaven to keep
your heart and mind, through anything and no matter what
comes.

—Patty Kemp

Prayer changes things, big-time! Those who live well the
inner Hope and power use prayer and faith to live every day op-
timistically, without worry or fear. In the midst of change, difficulties or success, they take refuge in the Divine, where they rest,
find peace and refreshment, discover new strengths. Alone time
with the Divine brings everything into proper perspective.

Those who shape a special life and an eternally enduring legacy of Hope follow Jesus' profound teaching to continually turn
inward—to distill, reflect, evaluate and commune in the private
inner room of the soul. The Divine Spirit is waiting patiently.

In prayer and meditation, we connect directly to the Divine's thoughts and ways. Meditation on higher thoughts nurtures the inner life of the spirit. A vibrant inner spirit-person is
one connected directly to the Divine. Through this connection
flows peace beyond understanding that keeps the heart calm and
quietly confident, even in troubled times. A sound mind grows
from an untroubled heart, inspired by Divine Wisdom.

Be still, rest your mind, listen to the beating of your heart,
find the peace from above that is undisturbed by worry. Breathe
in the peace, tranquility, strength and Hope of prayer and meditation on Eternal Truth.

Have daily devotions, prayer, Scripture reading and meditation in your home. Consider doing the same in your business by
promoting voluntary devotion groups for employees. For home
or business devotion settings, consider this format:

- Have one person read.
- Then have a group prayer, led by one person.
- Ask members of the group for their spoken requests. Those who do not want to make their requests public can simply indicate their request is to remain unspoken (unspoken to the group, but known to God and prayed for by the group leader as an unspoken request).
- Pray together, as a family or in your business.
- Pray for each other.

Peace of mind is found in praying and in releasing people, relationships, things and decisions to God, not in worrying and fretting over them.

HABIT 3
WORSHIP CORPORATELY

CAN'T YOU JUST STUDY, worship and pray on your own? Wisdom instructs clearly that we are to participate in regular local congregational worship services. You can and should study, worship and pray on your own as well.

HABIT 4
POSITIVELY AFFIRM OTHERS:
LOVE OTHERS AS YOU LOVE YOURSELF, AND
FORGIVE OTHERS AS YOU WANT TO BE
FORGIVEN

COMMUNICATE ACCORDING to Wisdom principles. The wise person who is humble and has a servant MindSet will always edify, build up and encourage others. This will be true in thought, word and action. Listen actively and respond with gentle care.

Adopt and always follow the Golden Rule of Wisdom. Defer, in your thoughts and behavior, to others' best interests. Treat others as you would want to be treated if your roles were reversed. Every time you make a decision and take action on it, first think in your heart how you would want the person you love most in the world to be treated by a stranger—then treat the other person in that way. That's the Golden Rule of Wisdom; it envisions always forgiving others unconditionally.

To help you form this habit, believe and put into practice these five Wisdom Truths:

1. *Don't hold to anger, hurt or pain. They steal your energy and keep you from love.*
                      —(personal paraphrase of) Leo F. Buscaglia

2. *I have decided to stick with love. Hate is too great a burden to bear.*
                      —(personal paraphrase of) Dr. Martin Luther King Jr.

3. *If you judge people, you have no time to love them.*
                      —(personal paraphrase of) Mother Teresa

4. *Whenever you are confronted with an opponent, conquer him with love.*
                      —(personal paraphrase of) Gandhi

5. *Goodness is not merely a beautiful thing but by far the most beautiful in the world.*
                      —(personal paraphrase of) Charles Kingsley

HABIT 5
DON'T WORRY

EASIER SAID than done?

How can you be at peace, free of anxiety?

Consider the methods and stories shared above at habit numbers 1 and 2.

Patty was concerned about Heather. She could not alter the situation, in her own power. She tapped the one power that indeed can change circumstances. She prayed and trusted God. *Then* peace came, you might say, on the wings of prayer.

Faith and worry are incompatible. Worry negates faith and vice versa. If you worry, you destroy the single-minded concentration it takes to follow Wisdom's instructions on faith, prayer and making choices based on the principles, values and priorities of Eternal Truth.

Wisdom's pages are clear that we are to give the cares of life to God, in faith through prayer. By *give* I mean in prayer time, we release our worries to the Divine and go our way in faith, knowing our concerns are in the most skilled Hands in the universe.

Another promise on the pages of Wisdom is that God always works out everything for good to those who are in harmonious, personal relationship and partnership with the Divine. It may not turn out the way we thought it should, but the Divine promises it will be good for all concerned. So as you pray and release worries to God daily, stand steadfast in faith on that promise.

I would be remiss if I didn't mention two additional thoughts on worry.

Often we worry over things that never could reasonably occur. Other times, we worry because we know the choices we have made and the actions we have taken were unwise. When Wisdom is not inside, fear causes great inner distress. Many respond to the distress by manipulating others and by behaviors that create problems or compound problems caused by unwise choices. Worry will not change a choice already made. Accompanied by unwise behavior, worry only assures things go from bad to worse.

In summary, instead of worrying or remaining anxious about anything, my suggestions are fivefold:

1. Read Scripture every day.
2. Release your concerns and cares to God through prayer that begins with thanksgiving; pray in faith to the Divine, believing that God works things out for good in His time; pray and receive the peace of God that comes on the wings of such prayer.
3. As you wait in faith, take Saint Paul's advice: Think on things that are good, noble and pure.
4. Go to the Appendix of this book and consider the thoughts shared under core belief 4 of the Philosophy of Wisdom.
5. Make spiritually wise choices.

NUGGET OF INSPIRATION

As we think in our heart, so we are.

—(personal paraphrase of) Solomon

CHAPTER TEN

GRACIOUS GOODNESS

The fruit of the Spirit is love, joy, peace, long-suffering, gentleness, goodness, faith, meekness, temperance.
　　　　　　　　　—(personal paraphrase of) Saint Paul

Reputation is what we appear to be from the outside looking in. Character is who we really are inside looking out.

When we live according to the Philosophy of Wisdom, our character is transformed. It is rebuilt with loving, God-like graces—as the Spirit of God comes to dwell in our inner spirit-person.

The change cannot help but display itself. Indeed, the graciousness of a radiant, shining personality is visible for all to see. This is Wisdom's amazing disposition: the mirror image of the Spirit of God living inside us, glowing out through our lives.

Wisdom's amazing disposition is seen outwardly as gracious goodness and as a pleasant, peaceable approach to life. The humility of mind can be seen in selfless, unbiased attitudes, and in just, kind and compassionate actions.

Those with Wisdom's amazing disposition command trust, because they share themselves and their blessings magnanimously and generously with others. And they are faithful and diligent, willing to sacrifice and eager to forgive; they are kind, merciful and patient; they are responsible communicators and possess great self-control.

All these qualities are expressions of God-like character and the HeartSkill of Wisdom.

Wisdom's amazing disposition manifests itself, inwardly and outwardly, as graciousness, the central grace of Wisdom's amazing disposition. Graciousness describes the inward and outward personality and disposition of the MindSet of Wisdom. If this graciousness seems almost too good to be true, that is because it comes from a supernatural Divine Source.

Virtues are qualities that we can develop by self-discipline and thus, can be solely a function of our own doing, as contrasted with God working in and through us.

Graces on the other hand are pure inner qualities that result from the Spirit of God living inside a reborn spirit. Thus, graces are not the result of what we can do on our own.

A grace yields superior results to a self-made virtue because of its power source. Graces equip, empower and motivate us to give graciously to others without regard to whether they deserve it or not. Graces equip, empower and motivate us to be merciful to others regardless of what they deserve.

It is very hard for an unwise heart to be merciful or gracious because these are unnatural responses. In contrast, a spiritually wise heart is ruled by Wisdom's motive (unconditional love) and passion (service to God and others before self). To the spiritually wise heart, mercy and grace are natural. We can trust our heart when it is full of graces because the Spirit of God dwelling inside gives us the integrity and honor of God, as the basis for their behavior. We cannot trust a self-serving mindset to direct the heart to be virtuous. Character will break down eventually, unless the inner spirit-person has attained a new heart and mind through spiritual transformation.

WISDOM'S POISE

INNER CALM, steadiness and peace are gifts to us from God that manifest outwardly as composure, serenity and gracious goodness. I refer to these as Wisdom's poise.

It does not matter what circumstances we face, we can face them and deal with them through the inner strength, courage and peace that come from the Spirit of God inside. These elements of Wisdom's poise are so powerful that sometimes they are beyond human understanding.

Serenity is calm in the midst of the storms of life. Inner spiritual serenity and composure are characterized by a peace of heart and mind that can be discovered only through achieving a harmonious relationship with God. Once that relationship is established, inner serenity, composure and peace are maintained by praying and releasing matters to God. Relationship first, then release. The peace of God will then see us through any situation, any decision and any storm—anything!

Wisdom's poise is a calm, balanced approach to life displayed as quiet, gracious and humble confidence. Wisdom's poise is possible once we have confidence in God and in Truth—not in ourselves or in philosophies of folly. It is not possible to have true inner peace and serenity if we continue to worry! Just as parents and grandparents watch over children, so God watches over us. Despite what philosophies of folly teach, spiritual serenity cannot be willed or intellectualized. God grants unto us peace of mind and heart as a gift of grace. We get something we do not deserve. There is nothing we can do to deserve God's grace. We cannot will it or create it with any amount of will power or intellect we have.

Wisdom's poise is a result of spiritual composure in the midst of the fears, storms and doldrums of life. It is key to conquering life's daily frustrations. It shows in everyday living and working. As inner grace manifests outwardly as gracious goodness, love, not fear, becomes the motive that controls our decisions.

Gracious goodness is seen outwardly as faith, courage, perseverance, forgiveness, humility, generosity, justice and compassion! I'll close this chapter with brief discussions of the first three of these personal virtues. The remaining five are discussed in a later chapter dealing with relationships.

FAITH

HAVING THE SUPERNATURAL faith and courage to take action or to refuse to act is one of the major graces that distinguish courageous people, those possessing Wisdom's poise.

Faith requires that we walk and live above our momentary circumstances seen with natural eyes. Faith is the hope beyond those circumstances. It is the hope our spiritual eyes see.

Our faith is made visible to us and others in the strength of our beliefs. What and whom we believe and trust is just as real as anything perceived with the natural eye or intellect. Sometimes faith is in the supernatural—something not yet seen or understood by our naturally limited faculties. Other times, faith is in something as easy to see as a check written one day and honored the next. We put our money and faith in the bank. We have confidence the bank will honor our check, and when it clears, our faith is honored and we no longer operate by faith! Our faith in God should be very great, since God can cover any "check" written on true faith. We understand little, if all we understand is what can be seen or explained. Truth originates and exists in the spirit world inside and outside us, out beyond the physical or intellectually comprehensible realms of our lives.

Faith is a matter of trust in another. Worry trusts only self. When we have done what we can, then is the time to remember that prayer, our invisible tool, can make a very visible difference. I encourage you to pray and stand still in faith, believing that God can and will work out any situation for good. Success or failure is less the result of what we do than of what we are inside at those crucial moments.

COURAGE AND PERSEVERANCE

COURAGE IS MENTAL or moral strength to venture, persevere and withstand danger, fear, difficulty, opposition and hardship. There are times in our lives when it takes courage just to survive. Harriet Beecher Stowe wrote, "When you get into a tight place, and everything goes against you, till it seems as though you could not hold on a moment longer, never give up then—for that is just the place and time that the tide will turn." People who display real courage place others first, always.

Those who have faith and absolute trust and take their refuge in and direction from God are able to overcome the world's backward paradigm for thinking, decision making and action—and the related destructive results. They display persevering passion in their beliefs, principles and values. Much of their success can be attributed to the faith that gives them courage to hang on long after others have let go. That becomes the birth of the third grace that must be possessed for us to survive in the very rough-and-tumble world: perseverance. Each of us can choose to become a person of absolute faith and trust in God. Each of us can choose Wisdom and Truth as the guide for our inner spirit-person. Each of us can choose to open ourselves to God's gifts of grace, passion and courage. We can choose!

The soil of enduring success is Wisdom. The seeds planted in that soil are our choices. And our faith, courage and perseverance are the roots, water and branches. A wise person whose heart is full of grace keeps the faith, endures, helps others when they stumble or become tired, weeps with those who weep, presses on. Charles Beard once said, "When it is dark enough, you can see the stars." And Jesse Jackson said, "Hold your head high, stick your chest out. You can make it. It gets dark sometimes but morning comes. . . . Keep hope alive." We can look at the sky and choose to see either the darkness or the brightness of the stars. When we choose to look at the stars, we express our faith that good will come and growth will occur in our lives and the lives of everyone we love. We can and should expect the best of things when walking the inner spiritual path to Wisdom, Honor and Hope.

When we are faced with adversity, how we handle the storm is far more important than mere survival. Endurance often means pain, sweat and tears. Family and others can throw harsh words at us, in anger. People can engage in many other destructive behaviors that can harm us and those we love. At times, there is no good reason for what happens. How we handle these situations is what counts. The present and eternal rewards of endurance are very worthwhile.

NUGGET OF INSPIRATION

THE SIMPLE PATH:
> The fruit of silence is prayer.
> The fruit of prayer is faith.
> The fruit of faith is love.
> The fruit of love is service.
> The fruit of service is peace.

—Mother Teresa

PART TWO

Relationship HeartSkill

CHAPTER ELEVEN

CONNECTING AT THE HEART

Seek first to understand rather than to be understood.
—(personal paraphrase of) Solomon

HUMANITY'S ONGOING QUESTIONS

HOW DO YOU HEAL hurts and disappointments? How can you save your dreams, your children, your relationships and your family? How can you move past blame, guilt and shame to freedom, excellence and success? How do you find balance in a teetering relationship? How can you keep from being destroyed by relationship problems, difficulties and breakups? How can you protect your children from these things? How do you break a chain of broken relationships? What can you change in order to be assured of having better relationships?

How can you regain self-respect and self-esteem? How can you stop worrying and losing sleep, and find that inner peace? How can you keep your family together? How can you avoid broken relationships or divorce? How can you stop using people? How can you permanently conquer feelings of shame, unworthiness, rage, anger, hate, jealousy, grief and loneliness?

The answers are not found in overintellectualizing the problems or the solutions. The answers are not found in self-directed and self-generated efforts. The answers are not found in philosophies of folly that teach the power of positive thinking, without teaching you how to change your inner spiritual database of thought. The name of the game is not how little we can give and how much we can get. That is an asinine approach to relationships, yet it is almost always the approach taken by those who embrace and practice the philosophies of folly, because the self-serving MindSet demands this approach.

The answers begin with fixing the inner spirit-person. Then the core solution is in place inside each person to help him or her handle problems in relationships, families and the workplace. When we view our roles, responsibilities and relationships through the inner spiritual lens of Wisdom, Honor and Hope, we see a completely different world than the one seen through the hopelessness of folly and the self-serving mindset. We will find the answers we seek by walking the inner path to true greatness and emulating wise, honorable and hopeful behavior models.

The MindSet of Wisdom can lead to the very best results in personal, family and work relationships. Our dreams and expectations can become realities, when we live and work every day according to the Philosophy of Wisdom, and put Wisdom's motive, passion, amazing disposition, and selfless gracious-servant principle into practical operation in our home and work environments.

When Wisdom, Honor and Hope bless your inner life, they will take hold in every aspect of your outer life, every role and relationship in your daily living and working. Your new self—spiritually motivated and inspired—seeks to uplift, support and love others in the same manner you would want for yourself, if roles were reversed.

PEOPLE AND RELATIONSHIPS MATTER MOST

MEANINGFUL, SUCCESSFUL relationships are shaped and nurtured when each party in a relationship is respectful, dutiful and accountable. Going far beyond the call of duty, doing more than others expect—this is what excellence is all about. This is what keeps relationships together and flourishing. Excellence in relationships comes from each party in a relationship striving, maintaining the highest standards, looking after the smallest important details (and overlooking the smallest unimportant details!) Excellence in relationships means caring—making a special effort to do more than was bargained for.

The way to pursue and attain excellence with distinction is through embracing and following the Philosophy of Wisdom.

- *If you believe that your power source is God,*
  then you will realize that all of his children are connected to you through Him—and this is the beginning of understanding.
- *If you believe that your life's purpose is serving God, loving Him and serving and loving others,*
  then you will seek to understand and support others—and this is the beginning of faithful service.
- *If you believe that you're both a spiritual and physical being,*
  then you gain a clearer perspective of the difficulties, celebrations, sorrows and ultimate triumph of humanity—and this is the beginning of compassion and abiding love.
- *If you believe that prayer is necessary and fulfilling,*
  then you will seek strength to keep serving, understanding and loving no matter the circumstances—and this is the beginning of peace.
- *If you believe that help and guidance are all around you,*
  then you will regularly tap into and share that guidance with others—and this is the beginning of ultimate joy.

The Philosophy of Wisdom is not intended to keep a believer on a mountaintop, separated from humanity, to praise the Creator in extended solitude. Rather it insists that we come down to our purpose and work at the foot of the mountain—where children are playing, whining and questioning; where the machinery of commerce, production and management are grinding with and against each other; where traffic snarls and paperwork test our spiritual outlook; where husbands and wives find themselves caught in daily routines, struggles and ordinariness. This place at the foot of the mountain—this place we call home, where life is happening—this is where we find the relationships within which we are to practice the Philosophy of Wisdom.

As my father used to tell me, a person with an experience is never at the mercy of a person with a theory. You have your own experiences of good and not-so-good relationships. You have your own unique feelings, emotions and thoughts about your relationships. The Philosophy of Wisdom's relationship truths, principles, values and priorities can help you improve all your relationships, most especially your close relationships—those with your family and coworkers. The relationship values and priorities of Wisdom have significance for the here and now—and into eternity. They are

> Faith, honesty and trustworthiness
> Justice, responsibility and commitment
> Sacrifice, diligence and patience
> Discipline, humility and harmony
> Faithfulness, courage and peaceableness
> Generosity, perseverance and fidelity
> Compassion, graciousness and loyalty
> Reverence, gentleness and kindness
> Wisdom, Honor and Hope

When you weave these values and priorities into your inner spirit life, their qualities will become the qualities you manifest in your outer life. You can then achieve true relationship excellence.

RESPONSIBILITY IN RELATIONSHIPS

THERE APPEAR TO BE three major types of responsibility in our relationships with others. The first is responsibility to ourselves. This includes all our personal choices, especially whether we choose to follow the path to Wisdom, Honor and Hope, or to follow the path of folly and ruin. It also includes expending effort to know ourselves—what we need, expect and want; what we like and don't like; what works for us and what doesn't. And it includes the responsibility we carry to share with others from our own experiences the truth about all these things, to show up and be authentic. Another part of our responsibility to ourselves is to choose purposefully, when we are performing our role in relationships.

We can be purposeful, that is, conscious of who we are and why we do what we do. Being purposeful can include choosing to walk the inner spiritual path to Wisdom, Honor and Hope in all our relationship roles and choices. Then our relationships will be harmonious and of the highest quality.

The second kind of responsibility is to the other person in the relationship. This includes giving others the space to be who they are, without our trying to control them, change them or limit their own ability to be responsible to themselves. Incumbent in this is seeing others as unique and precious children of God.

The third kind of responsibility in our relationships is to the relationship itself. The relationship is a separate and distinct entity from each person in the relationship. The relationship itself can be described as the shared consciousness and unconsciousness created when the persons in the relationship come together and interact. The words *synergic* and *dynamic* describe the actions and effects of relationship interaction. When the relationship and the behavior are based on and governed by Eternal Truth, synergy and dynamism are the positive results of people working together harmoniously in a more effective and productive way than would be true of the sum of their individual efforts.

THE SELFLESS GRACIOUS-SERVANT PRINCIPLE

THE CORE RELATIONSHIP principle of the MindSet of Wisdom is the selfless gracious-servant principle. This principle instructs us to serve the interests of others first and to treat others in relationships precisely as we would want to be treated. That principle can only be genuinely and continually operative based on Wisdom's inner character and integrity that manifest internally and externally as Wisdom's amazing disposition. Wisdom's amazing disposition is the key to building and maintaining unbroken, harmonious relationships. Wisdom-based relationships are all about the keen desire to understand what others need and the gift to pleasantly and profitably provide what they need. To accomplish that fulfillment, we must go beyond our natural self to reach out to others, seek to understand them and their concerns and truly care for them and their needs. This cannot be accomplished within our natural powers, skills, motives and desires. Our inner spirit-persons must receive supernatural guidance from the Divine inside, so that our motives and desires are wise, honorable and hope giving. Then, by following Wisdom's principles and using Wisdom's methods, we will be equipped with the powers and skills to find out what people need and give it to them.

OTHERS FIRST

THE PRIMACY OF LOVE—Wisdom's governing motive and dynamic for achieving and maintaining relationship synergy—is unsurpassed by any other power, method or means. *We must always keep in mind that what the other parties in our relationships cannot do for themselves is the reason they are in relationship with us.*

All parties to a relationship should bring good things from their individual perspectives. Wisdom instructs that we must do our part, regardless of what the other person or persons in the relationship do. Wisdom never gives to the other party based on what is given, but always gives according to what Wisdom requires.

For example, Wisdom walks very softly and carries no big stick. It never fights fire with fire or uses hurting and biting words to repay others for real or imagined injuries. We must always remember that relationships are a sacred trust and that, together, good things can happen for both parties only when they remain true to that sacred trust. Wisdom demands love without compromise, even to the unloving, and love in the most trying of relationship circumstances. There are no time-outs from Honor to allow us to speak harsh words and ask for forgiveness later.

Wisdom teaches that we always have to be there for the other party and that peace begins with a smile. Wisdom will not accept or entertain invitations to hatred or dissension. If we allow Wisdom to be our intelligence, then love and peace will triumph in our relationships. We can permit our love of others and our keen interest in others to develop in our relationships, so that our relationships grow strong enough to weather the differences of opinions, skills or ideas that inevitably arise. When our relationships are deep, and based on Wisdom, they become easier to sustain and more fruitful in every respect. Wisdom encourages us to overlook the other person's flaws, realizing that we all have our own flaws. We then see the good things in others and keep our thought lives and decision making on Wisdom's highest plane.

Wisdom's approach offers wonderful opportunities for sharing and growing together. Caring relationships have the best opportunity to be harmonious, unbroken and mutually profitable. Caring relationships are *not* a one-shot deal. They are continual building and maintenance projects that need large infusions of time and energy and that yield tremendously valuable results in our lives and in the lives of everyone we influence.

LOVE SERVES OTHERS

WISDOM TEACHES THAT LOVE serves others and is not selfishly self-serving. Wisdom *chooses* to honor and serve others, even if the only reward is the satisfaction of knowing that you chose to be thoughtful. Consider this story from my daughter, Heather, about thoughtfulness.

Some of my best memories result from the thoughtfulness of other mothers. One year on my birthday, my friend Sasha came to the office with her two children just to wish me a happy birthday. She had been rehearsing the song "Happy Birthday to You" with her oldest child, Natalie. Natalie sang the song especially for me. Although their visit was brief,

Sasha and Natalie's thoughtfulness meant so much. Sasha showed that she cared very much for me and for our friendship by planning something very special and driving twenty-five miles out of her way to do something nice for me.

Thoughtfulness like Sasha's is the result of selfless, gracious caring.

RUSTY'S LOYAL LOVE

THIS STORY IS ABOUT my son, James (we all call him Rusty), and his wife, Tracy. These two people have taught me a great deal about love, relationships, and Wisdom's amazing disposition. I have only known Tracy for a short time. But I have known Rusty all his life, and I'm only scratching the surface of the Wisdom lessons I have learned from Rusty during our twenty-four-year father-son relationship. The Wisdom I am writing about is experience-based, not simply philosophical. It is learned only in the real world, through living Wisdom's "real-deal," life-changing principles, which have no boundaries based on age, gender, economic status, position, title, race or nationality.

Yesterday: When They Were Young

IT WAS ABOUT 5:30 P.M. on the afternoon of September 20, 1997, when Rusty and Tracy took their marriage vows. The day of Rusty and Tracy's wedding was filled with joy and happiness. Hope was high within them as they considered their future together. But since their wedding day, they have faced a lot more than they would have imagined, even in their wildest dreams.

Less than two months after they married, an unexpected pregnancy turned into one of the most wonderful moments for them and for their family and friends. The joy in their faces and the love in their eyes were so touching on the night they came to our house to share their special news. Even though our daughter Heather, was just about to give birth to Justus, our first grandchild, the news of a second grandchild was just as exciting to Pops (me) and Patty (my wife).

Nobody knows why, but in a matter of days, Tracy's health

spiraled downward and she had a miscarriage. All of our sorrow when we heard the news was as fast-moving and hard-hitting as our joy had been when we first heard she was pregnant.

Such a traumatic event can be devastating to a young couple. Even some long-established marriages disintegrate in the face of either one partner's illness or the loss of a child. Rusty and Tracy were dealing with both. Rusty and Tracy, though, also had Wisdom's Hope and Wisdom's motive to hold them together.

Patty and I began to breathe a little easier as we realized the depth of their mutual commitment. Then, as if all that had happened in those two months were not enough to test this young couple, Tracy's health continued to decline. We were all very concerned about her health and about these two young and hopeful lives that had become one in marriage.

Tender Touch

TRUE TO THE WISDOM within him, Rusty abandoned work and all other outside concerns in order to focus his devotion on Tracy. The boundaries of their hopes that had so quickly expanded in the days leading up to their marriage and at the beginning of that pregnancy now suddenly contracted to the center. They concentrated on what was truly important and enduring in their lives. Talk about Wisdom and Honor! They had no passion for material things, just for each other's presence and touch. Their choices proved what really mattered to them—their relationship. At twenty-two and twenty-one years old, both were clearly very wise.

Surgery seemed to resolve Tracy's health problem and they moved into a condominium after spending nearly two weeks, at night, refurbishing it. They were so proud of their efforts. Within forty-eight hours after the excitement of moving in, they were confronted with new concerns about Tracy's health. (Rusty and I were working together at the time of the news; he dropped what he was doing and went home to be with Tracy.) The news could have caused the couple a financial worry fit and pity party good enough for a queen and king. But Tracy and Rusty, with Wisdom inside, clung to their Hope with Honor.

Tracy's health has come full circle. She's doing great, and so is their marriage. Rusty and Tracy's Wisdom-based relationship has already passed a difficult test, and it will continue to be strong, as long as these two wonderful young people base their decisions on Wisdom.

SHARE YOURSELF, YOUR LIFE

TRACY AND RUSTY learned that *being* precedes *doing*. Their relationship is more valuable than their wallet, their careers or any of their other dreams. As they should, and as we should, they put important things first: character, each other's well-being and their relationship. Becoming one is not Wisdom's desire solely for the marriage relationship. Wisdom believes this is the model for all relationships.

NUGGET OF INSPIRATION

For one human being to love another; that is perhaps the most difficult of all tasks, and the ultimate, the last test and proof, the work for which all other work is but preparation.
—Rainer Maria Rilke

CHAPTER TWELVE

CARETAKERS

People care about how much we care, far more than they care about how much we know.

—Cecil O. Kemp Sr.

THE CARETAKER OF A FAMILY OF FIVE SQUIRRELS

ON A RECENT early Sunday morning, I marveled as I observed a family of five healthy and happy squirrels playfully gamboling about in the front yard of our home—a huge manicured yard full of trees, with food, water and play opportunities in abundance. Winken, Blinken, Nod, Moe and Curly were absolutely having a ball as they ran and played.

Not one of the five squirrels appeared the least bit concerned with the things that consume most humans' time and attention. They were not busy chasing things so they would have more than others. During the entire time I watched, neither the family as a group, nor any individual squirrels, quarreled over territory, titles, money or possessions.

I did notice, however, that early on, Curly, God bless his little red curly-haired body, stood on his hind feet in the center of

our driveway, patiently waiting while the other four were running and playing. Curly seemed to be a one-squirrel family, at
first, politely asking to join the others. The other four noticed
Curly and ran back across the drive as if to say, "Come on, join
us, and let's be a family together." Curly was more than happy to
join, and the squirrels all became part of one big, happy family—
at least for that half hour.

As I watched, I could not help but think how their great
Caretaker must also be watching from above. Yet during the
thirty minutes or so that I observed them, Winken, Blinken,
Nod, Moe and Curly didn't stop even once to say thanks to their
Caretaker. The Caretaker provided their every need anyway because His motive was Wisdom's motive—He lovingly and humbly focused on caring and providing for these others first,
without expectation of thanks, and without putting Himself or
His personal interest first.

And I thought how this same great Caretaker is observing
us—caring for us with the same unconditional, limitless love. Yet
how he must rejoice when we acknowledge His guidance and offer gratitude for this earthly experience and the chance to create
and love within the rays of his Light. Incredibly, this great Caretaker has commissioned us to do His work, to care for others
and this earth, to love as He loves—unconditionally and without
limit. Wisdom teaches us this and instills in us this commission.
We are also caretakers whose motive and deep passions should
move us to act without personal interest. The MindSet, skill,
motive, passion, thought and power of our Caregiver, as well as
His caregiving strategy, were easy to discern on that squirrel-
watchin' day. He asks that we emulate this Divine work.

Our first priority should always be serving others. We should
follow the squirrels' Caretaker's caregiving strategy for best results in every aspect of our roles and relationships. Many people,
sad to say, function from a selfish and arrogant heart that creates
a self-serving mindset. Their strategy of action places priority on
themselves rather than on the needs and wants of others.

As I continued to watch the squirrel family, I began to ponder how so many of us use our intellect, our ability to reason and
our power of choice to manipulate people and situations and to

engage in other inappropriate, self-serving behavior. This is because we naturally want our needs and wants met first, and then and only then will we consider others' needs and wants.

I must be totally honest and tell you that I laughed aloud that Sunday morning when I thought about how much wiser Winken, Blinken, Nod, Moe and Curly were than most of us. Here were five creatures without the ability to think, reason or decide for themselves, and with a Caretaker much more powerful than they. Still they were the center of His attention. The squirrels gave no thought or energy to advancing their position or status or accumulating material possessions to establish dominance over each other. They were happy merely to enjoy the benefits of their Caretaker's attention.

Why isn't this the dominant picture seen daily in our families and communities? The caretaker in most situations is coming from the self-serving mindset. I know. I've been there and done that and, as you know, my results were far inferior to the squirrels' results!

TOUCHED BY EARTHLY ANGELS

Let parents bequeath to their children not riches, but the spirit of reverence.

—Plato

My father used to tell us stories similar to my squirrel story to help us understand Wisdom-based relationships and how the HeartSkill and MindSet of Wisdom functions in relationships. My father pointed me and my siblings toward simplicity, unconditional love and honor. "Practice those and everything else will take care of itself," was his advice. He and my mom were truly caretakers—they were concerned as much for our inner health as for our physical health—and they knew what tools to provide for lasting fulfillment. They also did not count their own cost to provide those tools.

Both of my parents knew that really caring means giving and sharing, and that's how they lived their lives. Full-time farming and full-time assembly-line jobs in an apparel factory filled their days, yet they still found time for great caring. They knew well that the best love is the love you give. They slept little and lived every waking moment for their children. My beautiful and athletic mother made time to teach me how to play baseball, basketball and football. My father diligently taught me how to manage money and take care of business. And instead of using what should have been spending money for themselves, they made sure there were special things for each child. Their careful management of the gains from cotton field and factory sweat assured us of never lacking for anything materially. More importantly, the dedicated time they gave each child every day taught us the personal, relationship, leadership, family and business values and priorities of the Philosophy of Wisdom.

My parents gave of *themselves,* not simply of things such as money or possessions. They were always going about the business of doing for others what others could not do for themselves. They did not give in order to receive. They gave and shared because the inner joy and happiness of helping others helped them as well as others.

A WORTHY MODEL

"IT'S NOT HOW MUCH you do, but how much love you put into doing," said Mother Teresa. "Don't give leftovers. And give until it hurts."

As I was writing this book, I prayed for guidance on whom to use as the ultimate caretaker model with Wisdom's amazing disposition. Whose life and work reflected unconditional love for everyone? The answer came back quickly and clearly—Mother Teresa, who made Calcutta her home and serving others her purpose. Mother Teresa was human, just like you and me. She faced the same choice we face, to embrace Wisdom or philosophies of folly. Clearly, Mother Teresa chose to follow Wisdom, and the rest, as they say, is history. And what a story it is!

Mother Teresa was perhaps the most important woman of the last hundred years, as well as one of the most admired people in all of history. She won the Nobel Peace Prize, and gave her financial reward, almost a half-million dollars, to the poor. She insisted that the customary awards banquet be skipped, so that the money normally spent on an expensive function for dignitaries could instead be given to feed the poor. Think about that for a moment. Think about how humble she was. I would have had a difficult time not wanting to strut around in front of the world at the awards banquet. Yet Mother Teresa never even considered that thought. She was too busy making sure others were cared for. Unconditional love in action!

She gave herself, sharing her very life with the poorest of the poor, India's so-called untouchables. She cared for people whose own relatives refused to come near them. She cared for the sick and the dying. She firmly believed Wisdom's basic truth—that we should love everyone—because of the value of each person to God. She thought it wrong to pay attention to any factor that might otherwise cause us to either favor or discriminate in choosing whom to love or not love. She never became inebriated with her power and influence, which were far greater than any of us are likely ever to possess. She always expressed appreciation to those who gave money to her effort, but her selfless devotion to the people she helped demonstrated to millions of people the great importance of sharing time and one's self.

Mother Teresa used her power and influence only for the good of those she served. It has been said that her seeds of love, grace and generosity led to the largest harvest of compassion seen in our world in a long, long, long time. She definitely made this world a better place in which to live. Mother Teresa said she was called to serve the King of the Universe. Serve she did! Her heart, hands, feet and every fiber of her being were focused on serving others first. Her reward had eternal significance. Mother Teresa left enduring footprints on the sands of time, and yet she was so humble that to call her sublime would be an understatement of the graciousness and Wisdom in her heart.

The source of Mother Teresa's graciousness was the grace of God. This grace was constantly replenished by prayer and by action done for Love. God is Love, so that Love was the source of Mother Teresa's graciousness.

God is the source of graciousness for all with Wisdom inside them. *Agape,* as mentioned earlier in this book, is used to refer to God-like love. Saint Paul instructs us that unconditional *agape* in us is the source of the inner character graces of humility, patience, loyalty, faithfulness, trust, peace, justice, compassion, forgiveness, generosity, diligence, sacrifice and responsibility.

I consider it an honor and privilege in my life to have turned back to Wisdom and to share the Source of Mother Teresa's inspiration.

NUGGET OF INSPIRATION

I used to ask God to help me. Then I asked if I might help Him. I ended up by asking Him to do His work through me.
—Hudson Taylor

CHAPTER THIRTEEN

SHINING STARS

(with excerpts from the book *I Know Who I Am,* by Lesa Renee)

☆ ☆ ☆

Now I ask you, dear children,
Do you know who you are?
You're as bright as the brightest,
Heavenly star . . .

☆ ☆ ☆

Two of the most important children born in the last hundred years happen to be my grandson, "Justus Squirrel," and my granddaughter, "Jessi Squirrel." How do I know they're so special? Simple! I'm their Pops! (You may want to write me for a special collage of pictures of Justus and Jessi. They are free, *and* you will also receive a couple of five-hour videos and a few lengthy audiotapes, all about Justus and Jessi, with Pops as your host.)

POPS'S STORY

AT 8:40 A.M. on December 26, 1997, our first grandson was born. Justus Squirrel weighed a little more and was a little longer than a baby (or an adult) squirrel. We could tell almost immediately that he was built more like his father, Chris, than like his mother (our daughter, Heather), since he weighed almost eight pounds and was twenty inches long. That's a little more than 8 percent of Heather's normal weight but 33 percent of her height! He definitely looks just like his Pops (me, in case you missed that!), except when he cries. Then, of course, he behaves like somebody else.

When Justus grows up, he'll be like his dad. He will also be like his Uncle Rusty. And most importantly, he will be like his Pops (me, in case you missed that again). He will likely be the same size as his dad (six feet tall, with 225 pounds of solid muscle) and will undoubtedly follow in his dad's wrestling shoes and be acclaimed USA's High School Wrestler of the Year. (By the time Justus was two weeks old, Chris already had him benchpressing over a hundred pounds at the gym. And Justus drives himself there every day, of course.)

His size will help him follow in his Uncle Rusty's baseball shoes to win USA's Player of the Year and MVP honors at the College World Series. Justus will hit .600 his senior year at Cow College (his Pops's alma mater, of course) and set a new record by batting 1000 at the College World Series. In every game of that series, Justus will throw out every runner who attempts a steal. As the catcher for Mississippi State, Justus will make a bases-loaded triple play to end a ninth-inning rally by Ole Miss and preserve State's championship 1–0 victory.

How? You want to know how? I have a couple of spare tickets to that game. Meet me in Omaha in late spring of 2018 and see for yourself! You can even catch the press conference the next morning, when Justus will announce he's signing with the Texas Rangers for $1 billion and will go straight to the majors to replace an aging "Pudge" Rodriguez. He will also apologize to the fans in New York, Atlanta and L.A. for turning down much better financial offers there for the opportunity to be mentored by the best catcher in major league history.

And Justus will absolutely cherish his little cousin, Jessi Squirrel, born at 7:03 P.M. on March 10, 1999. Jessi is "very beautimous" like Tracy her mother and her Big Moms (Patty and Debbie) and her aunts, Tina and Heather. Jessi has dark wavy hair like her dad, Rusty—and like what her Pops once had (me in case you forgot who her Pops is). Jessi is already driving herself to the nursery each day (and on weekends to the mall). Jessi will grow up to be a mighty prayer warrior like her mom and like Aunt Heather and Big Mom Patty. And ten years from now, at age eleven, she will be the prettiest and smartest girl in her high school graduation class.

Jessi will graduate summa cum laude from Cow College, just like her bestest cousin Justus. That year she will be crowned Ms. Tennessee and Ms. America. As all young men will want to be like Justus Catcher of the Texas Rangers, all young women in America will model Miss America Jessi's lifestyle.

Okay, okay, I'll stop doting!

As you can see, I love my grandkids! And I love that my own kids—whom I dearly love—love my grandkids! I'm thrilled that they'll be raised in homes that see children as Shining Stars straight from heaven! This is what life and love and purpose— what living with meaning—is all about. So forgive an ol' Pops his gushing! What is certainly true is that, if their parents and grand-parents light them and equip them with spiritual roots and wings of truth, Jessi and Justus will have lives and lifestyles that others will want to model. Because those lives will be expressive of Divine Truth, of the Spirit of God within them.

HEATHER'S STORY

MY DAUGHTER, Heather, has some wise stories to share. They are starring—you guessed it— her son, Justus Squirrel.

True love is inexhaustible: The more you give, the more you have. And if you draw from the true fountainhead, the more water you draw, the more abundant the flow.
                                        —Antoine de Saint-Exupéry

When I became a mother, love took on a whole new meaning. If you are a parent or a grandparent, I bet you know exactly what I mean. I can honestly say that Justus's love for me, and mine for him, have taught me what it really means to love unconditionally.

Unconditional love accepts everyone in the same way as one accepts a little child like Justus. Unconditional love demonstrates the belief that God created every person as unique and precious. Unconditional love is just, without bias or regard for any factor, including anyone's circumstances, status or behavior. Unconditional love recognizes no limits. Unconditional love knows there is no such thing as excessive love.

I try to show unconditional love to my child by making him feel very special always. This special love and attention will prepare him to excel in life and to deal with life's ups and downs. I believe that an inexhaustible supply of unconditional love will assure your children of having lives full of significant meaning and purpose.

—Heather

To simplify means to eliminate the unnecessary so that the necessary may speak.

—Hans Hofmann

For some reason, many tend to think that the more intricate and elaborate something is, the better it is. Simplicity does not seem to be a real popular concept in the modern world. We have programmed ourselves to think that the more out of control—the fancier, the more decorated, or the more expensive—the better something will be.

I have learned, through Justus, that the opposite is the truth. True beauty only shines through when simplicity rules. There is nothing more wonderful than sitting on an unmade bed in the mornings with Justus and Chris, just sharing some hanging-out time. Most of the time we do not even have toys on the bed. Princess, our Maltese, will usually be on the bed with us, too. It is a lot of fun to watch how fascinated Justus becomes with her. Very simple, but I would not give up that time for anything.

Justus, as you have learned, has his adoring Pops and me "held hostage," on call, on demand, with that beautiful smile and his baby-blue eyes that are just like his dad's. Pops says grandparenting is as close to heaven as he's ever been! (You couldn't tell from his gushing, could you?!) Justus has shown us the beauty and joy of simplicity and the unconditional love that makes it possible.

—Heather

☆ ☆ ☆

I'll grow to move mountains,
I'll stand straight and tall,
I'll let my light shine,
And if ever I fall . . .
I'll grow even stronger,
Knowing just where I stand . . .
With God deep inside me,
I know who I am!

☆ ☆ ☆

BRIGHT LIGHTS

Children are the living messages we send to a time we will not see.

—Neil Postman

Helping a child reach his or her potential may require time, effort and emotional trials. But serving as guides and mirrors—reflecting God's hope, love and special plans for each of these special hearts—is a reward no other endeavor offers!

Parents have the choice and the opportunity to make a positive or negative difference in this world, especially through the influence of their lives on their children. The habits that consume our time, skills and other resources teach our priorities to our children and to other people we influence. Our choices demonstrate what we really believe and value. That is why it is so important for our beliefs and values to be guided by Wisdom, rather than folly.

Wisdom teaches us to place a high priority on our children. If we want our children to know that they are our Shining Stars, we need to set the kind of example that demonstrates the high priority we place on their well-being. We can choose to run our lives in overdrive, preoccupied with the unimportant pursuits of folly, or we can choose to spend more time with our children, doing things with them. We can play ball, have a tea party, swim, ride bikes, read, take a walk, clean out a closet or just do nothing together, sharing "hang time." The activity is not as important as the choice to spend time together.

APPRECIATION AND RECOGNITION

EVERYONE HAS the desire to be genuinely appreciated and praised, and children are no exception. You can help your children feel good about themselves by being generous with your kind words and recognizing your children's accomplishments.

Wise people make it their business always to show their genuine appreciation for others. Oftentimes, the one thing that will get a person to their goal is a little bit of sincere praise and encouragement! Kind words and praise cost nothing. They accomplish much. Few things in this world are more powerful and lasting than a word of genuine encouragement or sincere praise. Genuine encouragement and praise improve results by uplifting people, giving them that extra, soft push they need to make it through the task at hand.

Think of how you can give your children—and everyone else with whom you come in contact—genuine encouragement and praise, every day.

CONFIDENCE

WHEN WE OR OUR children walk into a situation where we know others are looking down their noses, for whatever reason, the manner in which we or our children allow that unwise way of thinking to affect us will either make us or break us. If we or our children permit others' unwise attitudes to control our confidence, we put ourselves into the inferiority-complex, fear-of-mistakes state of mind. Then we cannot hope to achieve excellence and lasting success.

Confidence comes from the inside, not from others or from external conditions! When our children come to us because they do not feel good enough to be in the presence of a particular person or they feel inferior to someone else, consider reminding them of these words of Eleanor Roosevelt: "No one can make you feel inferior without your consent." And be sure to share with them that the beginning point of their confidence is inside!

HOMES ARE BUILT OF LOVE

HOUSES ARE MADE of brick and mortar—a home is built of love. Wisdom teaches us that love can exist in every kind of family. Ideally, a father and a mother who follow Wisdom raise their children together in mutual love and support. But sometimes, family circumstances dictate that grandparents must raise their grandchildren, or a single father or mother must raise his or her children without the love and support of a spouse. Foster parents care for children who don't live with their birth families for all kinds of reasons. Fortunately, even a family that does not have ideal circumstances can create a loving home for the children by following the principles of Wisdom.

My friend and fellow author, Carl DeVilbiss, offers valuable insight into wise parenting—no matter the home circumstances.

Children and Troubled Relationships

Most people cherish their children. But in a troubled relationship, the interests of children can take second place to anger, blame and pain.

I have learned, as a divorced parent myself, that most people have a hard time recognizing when they are paying more attention to their own interests than to their children's. Some parents even use their children to punish their former partners, deliberately or inadvertently. Custody battles, for example, are frequently driven by hostility, rather than by Wisdom. Denying visitation to or speaking critically of an absent parent can damage both children and parents.

A relationship that involves children never really ends; it just changes its nature. Parents must reassure their children that they will always love and support them. Your conduct with your children's other parent is a powerful teaching tool.

You can choose to model the wise behavior that will help your children be confident that they are loved.

For the sake of your children's well-being, put the past behind, embrace forgiveness and conduct a harmonious relationship with your children's other parent. Walk in Wisdom, Honor and Hope, and give your children positive life lessons that will help them become successful adults.

Positive Life Lessons for Your Children

Model responsible behavior.

Children learn discipline by observing the consequences of their own and others' behavior. Wise parents teach their children the difference between discipline, which is ideally self-generated and based on Hope, and punishment, which is imposed from without and based in fear.

Troubled relationships cause fear and pain for everyone involved, including children. There are appropriate and inappropriate behaviors that can express emotional hurt. Allowing your children (or yourself) to act out inappropriately because of suffering teaches your children an unwise lesson: that wrong behavior is acceptable if you are in pain.

Being disciplined by our parents when we are children—and observing how our parents discipline themselves—is how most of us learn to distinguish appropriate from inappropriate behavior. Wisdom calls for parents to be fair and consistent in disciplining their children, regardless of circumstances. You can give your children the gift of Hope in difficult times by exercising consistent, fair discipline and by modeling wise self-discipline.

Show your humanity.

Parents are human beings with all the possibilities, responsibilities and contradictions that characterize the human condition. Showing your humanity to your children sets a very loving example by demonstrating that authenticity is safe, that there is no need to be other than who you are and that it is not necessary to wear a mask. You teach your chil-

dren that being aware of each other's strengths and weaknesses can contribute to a harmonious relationship. This is part of modeling how to be an effective adult.

Showing your children your humanity, your faults and weaknesses, your fears and feelings, your confusion and struggles in hard times, your disappointments and defeats, demonstrates that less-than-perfect people can still be worthy of loving relationships. Be open with your children about your humanity, in an age-appropriate and hopeful way, and you will help them learn to build strong relationships in the future.

Be honest.

I once thought I had to put on a neutral face to be a good parent, even when I was trembling inside. One day, my little daughter asked me why I was sad. My first thought was to assure her that I wasn't sad, but I realized she already knew I was, or she wouldn't have asked. So I shared with her what was going on with me. Now she is comfortable telling me how she feels, too.

Parents who are honest with their children about their feelings, in an appropriate way, give their children permission to have and express their own feelings in a healthy way. This gift of emotional validation can improve your children's lives and your relationship with them. Wise parents know that children recognize truth in their hearts.

Keep your promises.

A child's trust is a blessing that presents a parent with tremendous opportunities for good. Wisdom Truth tells us that we have the responsibility to influence our children's mindsets toward honorable and hopeful actions. Children are born with an innate ability to trust their parents and to trust God, but can lose that trust if they observe untrustworthy behavior.

It is tempting to make promises to children to gain their favor. Telling a child you are going to do something, and then not doing it, is as wrong and damaging as breaking any other business or personal contract. If a broken promise is not dis-cussed and corrected and amends made, the lesson delivered is that breaking promises is okay. That is a powerful lesson in wrong behavior.

—Carl DeVilbiss

Carl and Heather's words are so important—especially for today's culture where the material is often valued more than the spiritual.

Parents' wise examples help children prepare for and find a hopeful future and ensure that their lives will have significance and meaning. Our example is the primary way children learn to be adults. They learn far more from our actions than our words. Our actions show what we really believe. Children learn values and priorities from observing what we care about, how we act and how we handle mistakes and change. Living models of truth reveal God to our children and mold their hearts and minds so they can be Shining Stars lighting up their world with hope, kindness, honor, dependability and love. Priceless wisdom and beautiful memories are the rewards parents and children reap when parents invest their time in their children.

LIGHT THEM UP

FROM OUR EFFORTS, the world gains the next wave of Shining Stars. Wise seeds of time and example planted in our children's lives will blossom and shine, becoming the next wave of beautiful flowers and Shining Stars that brighten and light up the world.

We begin by seeing newborns as the Divine sees them. Each new child is unique, a very special Shining Star in God's eyes. Unqualified uniqueness and nearly limitless potential live in every child. When we recognize, encourage and nurture the uniqueness of every child, we give them roots to dig deep and wings to soar high and land safely. The truly wise adopt that view and never, ever change it. They seek to provide roots and wings and teach children to listen to the beat of that different drummer, allowing God's purpose for their life to be fulfilled.

With roots and wings, our children have a strong sense of who they are and the power to take them to the places they were created to go. Then these Shining Stars soar, see bright horizons and land safely as they pursue their grandest dreams.

Some final words from Heather: "My husband, Chris, and I have decided that the most valuable lesson we can share with our son is teaching him God's eternal purpose for his everlasting life. We intend to share the Philosophy of Wisdom and Wisdom Truth with him, and by our personal examples, live each day, walking the Inner Path to True Greatness."

☆ ☆ ☆

"I know who I am!"
Sang the soul with delight . . .
They rejoiced, she and God,
On that bright shiny night.

☆ ☆ ☆

NUGGETS OF INSPIRATION

Children are the hands by which we take hold of heaven.
—Henry Ward Beecher

My hope for my children must be that they respond to the still, small voice of God in their own hearts.
—Andrew Young

CHAPTER FOURTEEN

REACHING OUT

Divine love expressed through humans is the seed of mass epidemics of hope. All the flowers of all the tomorrows are in the seeds of today.

—Chinese Proverb

In an earlier chapter I cited eight outward expressions of the gracious goodness that results when we possess the HeartSkill and MindSet of Wisdom. These expressions are faith, courage, perseverance, forgiveness, humility, generosity, justice and compassion. In that earlier chapter I discussed the first three; in this chapter I discuss the last five.

THE OLIVE BRANCH

WISDOM TEACHES the complete antithesis of the model many follow in their roles and relationships. People under the influence of philosophies of folly cling to their hurts, become embittered, quarrel and destroy each other over slights, insults and injuries. How much better their lives could be if they chose to embrace Wisdom instead, with its simplicity and power of forgiveness.

Wisdom says we should be quick: Be first to forgive, and

keep on forgiving. Be liberal and magnanimous in forgiving others. Always extend the olive branch. When we ask how often we should forgive someone, Wisdom's pages tell us seventy times seven, each day! Unforgiveness widens the gap in tattered or broken relationships, regardless of the source of the conflict. This means that forgiveness is absolutely necessary to heal and preserve our significant relationships.

Wisdom is also clear on how to initiate the forgiving process, and who should go first. When we remember we have something against someone, or someone has something against us, Wisdom instructs us to go to that person and ask for forgiveness. This may seem unorthodox, but the benefits from applying it are astounding! Wisdom teaches us to adjust our attitudes by forgiving other people completely, regardless of what they did to us or said about us. Wisdom instructs us to get in the habit of dealing with our own baggage of unforgiveness and to do so in Wisdom's way. Wisdom's pages do not say that we should forgive only if we "feeeeel" like it. They say that you don't get *your* forgiveness without first producing forgiveness toward the *other person*. If you're in the habit of carrying grudges, you can choose to lose that bad habit and forgive others in Wisdom's way!

LET IT GO AND MOVE ON

The weak can never forgive. Forgiveness is the attribute of the strong.
—Gandhi

Forgiveness is an act of the will, and the will can function regardless of the temperature of the heart.
—Corrie Ten Boom

Really forgiving is forgetting what you forgave. Mercy and grace will be shown to you as you show them to others.
—(personal paraphrase of) Saint Paul

A spiritually wise heart leads us, promptly and willingly, to account for our mistakes and injustices. It also causes us to realize that forgiveness is the work of the Divine. When we are inspired by the Divine within, we choose to make amends and achieve reconciliation. Then, we can let the past sleep, so the future can awaken! Allowing God to work within us, we can initiate limitless forgiveness, make amends, restore, heal and effect true reconciliation.

We have to choose to let the other person off the hook and work out a way to get along with that person. It's as simple as that—or it's as complex and destructive as unforgiveness can be. Wisdom inside us will enable us to develop the self-discipline to be forgiving. We can accomplish much more with forgiveness than with bitterness and resentment. True resolution of conflict can happen only when Wisdom's motive (unconditional love) and Wisdom's passion (serving others) reign in our hearts. Healing relationships start with forgiveness.

When I was a boy, my maternal grandfather, Papa Adcock, once banned my father from Papa's home for what seemed like a trivial reason. After weeks of not seeing our entire family, Papa walked more than five miles to our house, apologized and asked forgiveness. He went home a happy man, leaving behind a happy family who immediately resumed daily visits to Papa's home. What does this story tell us about Wisdom? That when we forgive, or ask for forgiveness, in Wisdom's way, we become instruments of healing. Learn today to forgive—Wisdom's way. Learn to ask for forgiveness—Wisdom's way. Any other way leads to bitterness and destruction.

HUMILITY

WISDOM INSTRUCTS that the servant attitude is to be our mind's attitude. This can only be true if we have spiritually new and wise hearts. When reborn spiritually, each of us has a new heart with the potential to be a spiritually wise heart because the Spirit of God dwells in us. When the Spirit of God is in control of our inner being, our heart will be spiritually wise. It is natural then that a servant's attitude will be the dominant attitude of the inner spirit-person's mental sphere.

Saint Paul teaches us that we must not be selfish, not live to make a good impression on others, but instead be humble, thinking of others as no less than ourselves. We must not think only about our own affairs, but be keenly interested in others, so much so that we are motivated to attend their best interests. This humble servant attitude is ready, willing and able to prefer others before self.

GENEROSITY

LIFE'S BLESSINGS are not a measure of who we are, but of who God is. A sharing heart is one marked by evidence of Wisdom at work. Notice, I used the word *sharing*. I found during my years away from Wisdom that giving was easy. But a gift without the giver is empty. Those who share themselves with others achieve far better and enduring results than those who simply give money or empty words of praise.

Generosity is defined by Webster's New World Dictionary as "unselfishness: the quality of being generous, liberal, and magnanimous." Generous people who are rightly motivated share freely, with no strings attached, as an expression of thankfulness and gratitude for their own blessings. The best love is the love we share without expecting recompense. The motive that moves us to generosity is Wisdom's motive, which is unconditional love.

Right motive can be in control only when we have the right attitude toward sharing. Wisdom instructs us that we are not to give grudgingly or by necessity, but only because we truly want to, as a demonstration of the fact that we have been blessed. That's what sharing means.

Wisdom also instructs us to be cheerful givers. When we share with others, we are to share joyfully and willingly, with no expectation of thanks, no expectation of any kind of recompense. We are to share out of pure love. Unconditional love moves us to go beyond giving, to be joyfully willing to share generously. That is why the word *generous* is often used to describe a person's gracious attitude, an attitude that overlooks injury and insult, an attitude that rises above pettiness and meanness.

Wisdom instructs that we are blessed so that we can be a blessing to others. It teaches us that we must not withhold good from those to whom it is due, when it is in the power of our hand to give and share. Saint Paul said there should be reciprocity: when you have abundance, you can supply others' needs; when you have a need and they have abundance, they can supply your need. When you are adequately provided for, then the excess should be shared and used for enduring purpose in others' lives.

Sharing is the essence of what it means to have a servant attitude. Instead of hoarding or becoming prideful of our money and possessions, or misusing our status, power, time and talents as if we got them through our own power, we should be generous. God's blessings to us should be our motive for being generous with our love, mercy, loyalty and faithfulness to others.

OUR INNER SPIRITS ARE LINKED

WISDOM INSTRUCTS that we take care of one another, that we belong to each other and need each other. In other words, we are not islands to ourselves. Wise King Solomon notes on the pages of Wisdom how scary, risky and devastating it can be to try to go it alone, especially when faced with the storms of life such as the death of a loved one or health problems. He then contrasts being alone to the strength of a double- or even triple-braided cord. The point Solomon illustrates is very important to us. We need to look for opportunities to help everyone within our spheres of influence, and then, when we find out what they need, we must reach out and help them. It's as simple as that.

LINKED—NOT LOCKED

WE CANNOT REACH OUT to others, and have truly healthy relationships, until we ourselves have achieved threefold independence (spiritual, emotional and intellectual) of other people. A relationship in which a person hangs on to dependent behaviors (spiritual, emotional or intellectual) is not a truly healthy or whole relationship.

I am not suggesting notions such as self-dependence or independence from God. Only with the inner spiritual qualities of Wisdom, Honor and Hope can we have threefold independence and eliminate the games people play with each other in roles and relationships. Wisdom, Honor and Hope, as the basis of each person's responsibility to the other and to the relationship, create a whole, healthy relationship of true and highest-quality interdependence.

Am I suggesting that personal and relationship wellness is solely a matter of the spiritual realm? Of course not! I am a big believer in the value and importance of health-care professionals and institutions. I believe God gave us many wonderful doctors, scientists and organizations that have helped people recover from illnesses, such as depression. Nevertheless, I do believe that all healing starts in the heart of the inner spirit-person and works its way to the mind, rather than the other way around. Total healing of the inner spirit-person's heart begins with having the wise source of inspiration. When that source is God, and when we truly come into harmonious, personal, inner spiritual relationship with God, that spiritual balance leads to radical changes in our emotional, mental and physical wellness.

JUSTICE

JUSTICE IS A GRACE easier to proclaim than to define or clarify. Practicing it is even more difficult than proclaiming or defining it. Those who learn to practice it have learned to live wisely. When we are just, we have a deep, firm and constant desire to render to everyone that which is due them. Justice is the application of Truth to our daily lives. Wisdom says that doing rightly and justly is more acceptable than sacrifice. This is a clear proclamation that living justly is more important than any ritualistic correctness we may practice. Wisdom teaches us that being just means to treat others as we would want to be treated if our roles were reversed. Wisdom instructs us that we are not to be "respecters of persons." This means we are not to consider one person more important than another. We are not to be partial; rather, we are to give respect to all.

It is easy to see that people who are the objects of prejudice and intolerance suffer untold damage. What many don't realize is that great damage is suffered by those who cause injustice, who show partiality and disrespect. These people, by practicing prejudice, indelibly scar their inner spirit-person.

In Plato's *Republic,* Thrasymachus expresses the view that justice is nothing more than the interest of the stronger. All too often, this is what we call human justice: might makes right. With human justice, a weaker person is dominated by a stronger person, and the stronger person thinks, "You're getting exactly what you deserve." Human justice is practiced by people giving others what they "deserve," according to selfish motives. But that is human justice, not Wisdom's justice.

Wisdom's justice protects the interest of neither the weak nor the strong. Right interest is the interest of Wisdom's justice. Wisdom's justice does not rely on might to make right. It depends on the fruit of the Spirit of God manifesting in the lives of both the weak and the strong.

A truly just person is compelled by the right motive of love for others. This love manifests Wisdom's nature and character, not by giving others what they deserve from a human perspective, but what they are due according to Wisdom. Does this remind you of Mother Teresa's graciousness?

COMPASSION

How far you go in life depends on your being tender with the young, compassionate with the aged, sympathetic with the striving and tolerant of the weak and strong. Because someday in your life you will have been all of these.
—George Washington Carver

Wisdom has recorded on its pages a story commonly referred to as the Good Samaritan. What did the Good Samaritan do differently from the priest, the Levite or, for that matter, so many of us when we see hurting people? The Samaritan took time to determine the needs of a hurting, half-dead man by the road; he responded with true compassion from his heart and wallet, not with a bunch of nice-sounding, empty words. The Good Samaritan was not too greedy or too busy working in his own selfish interest, as the Levite was; he was not too busy, either, pretending to be wise, as the priest was.

The Good Samaritan took the time to attend to a crucial matter. He used his power, time, talents, money and possessions on the truly important things in life. He personally attended to the man's wounds. Then the Good Samaritan took the time to find this hurting man a room for the night at an inn. He personally transported the man to the inn and paid for a night's stay. Then he did something unheard of. The Good Samaritan gave the innkeeper a blank check to cover the stranger's stay, if one night was not long enough for the injured man to recover.

This would have been a remarkable enough story had the two men been relatives or friends. But they were total strangers. And even more remarkable, given the storyteller and His audience, the injured man was assumed to be a Jew from Jerusalem. According to John 4:9, Jews had no dealings with Samaritans. Despite this social barrier, the Samaritan responded to the victim he encoutered out of unconditional love, demonstrating Wisdom's selfless gracious-servant principle.

The answer to fear is love, not logic. The Samaritan could have reacted to the situation on the basis of historic prejudice, answering fire with fire. He could have supported this response with logic: Jews are my enemies; this man is a Jew; therefore, this man is my enemy. Instead the Samaritan responded by seeing the man and his need; he acted out of reverence for the God who had created both of them. Let's learn to start each day by saying, "God, if someone in my vicinity needs help today, help me to be the one who sees the need and reaches out to help."

REACHING DOWN AND REACHING UP

MOTHER TERESA thought we could all learn a great deal about life and relationships from the poor, if we would spend a little time with them and listen. She would tell how an Australian Aborigine refused to disclose who had brutally beaten him. The officials said that disclosing the offenders' identities would bring them to (human) justice. The Aborigine replied simply, "If you punish them, that will not heal my wounds."

This demonstrates both justice and compassion, Wisdom's way. Every time I have thought of or actually tried to get, revenge, invariably I am the one who gets hurt the most, especially inside. Wisdom leads us away from such destructive behavior—and the wise know why. Those who embrace and practice folly usually don't understand this, so they continue to seek revenge and pay the price for ignoring Wisdom.

Once, during her daily rounds in the city of Calcutta, Mother Teresa found a dying woman in the street. Her body was infested with worms, and she suffered from a gangrenous leg that had obviously been gnawed more than a little by rats. It was reported that Mother Teresa picked the woman up and carried her back to the Home for the Dying and for the Abandoned. There Mother Teresa bathed the woman in warm water and put her into a warm and clean bed. As she fought for her life, the dying woman said to Mother Teresa that she had lived "like an animal on the streets" and that she had never enjoyed such fine accommodations ever before in her life. "Now I can die like a human being," she said, "surrounded by love."

The seeds that Mother Teresa sowed day after day were the seeds of justice and compassion for people. And her humble and generous attitudes were the result of the graciousness at the center of her MindSet of Wisdom. The radiance and passion shining through her were a consequence of the inner character and integrity built inside her by Wisdom, its principles, its values and the Spirit of God alive and working through her. She beautifully displayed Wisdom's motive and passion.

Mother Teresa was not interested in words, and did not ask for them. She asked for a show of love through deeds. Her life, her passion, her very being, were dedicated to the service of others. She reached up to God, who in turn reached down to her; together they reached out to others.

Only Wisdom's motive and passion inside us can empower and motivate us to demonstrate that how much we care is more important than how much we know, what title we have or how many material possessions we have accumulated. You can choose right now to reach out and touch people with your love, mercy, grace, justice and compassion. Your example can inspire everyone around you to serve others unselfishly. Your relationships can heal and flourish when you walk in Wisdom's way.

NUGGETS OF INSPIRATION

Long is the road that has no turning lane.

—Cecil O. Kemp Jr.

The windows of my soul I throw
Wide open to the sun.

—John Greenleaf Whittier

CHAPTER FIFTEEN

THE POWER OF WORDS

Life and death are in the power of the tongue.
A soft answer turns away anger and strife.
—(personal paraphrase of) Solomon

STICKS AND STONES

AS CHILDREN WE SAID that "sticks and stones may break my bones, but words can never harm me." But this saying is far from the truth—it denies the powerful mental, emotional and spiritual impact of words. Wisdom teaches us that words are a power unto themselves. Word power is subordinate to the power of choice. We can choose how we will use the power of words, wisely or unwisely.

Unfortunately, many people are irresponsible and use their tongues destructively, demanding their way in communication with others and disregarding the potential for harm in their own words. An unwise and irresponsible person doesn't realize there is no gain—but a lot of potential loss—from a flow of uncontrolled, loosely spoken words. Unwise people, guided by the self-serving mindset, will listen little, speak too frequently and often ignore the importance of timing—when and how they communicate. The person with a self-focused mind rarely sees the point in guarding his or her conversations carefully. These people often fail to realize that silence is sometimes the best response. Whatever the cost, to themselves and others, unwise and irresponsible people will speak first and consider the consequences later.

The words we use, the manner of our expression and the timing of what we say all can be either constructive or destructive in our personal and professional roles and relationships. Words have consequences in the actions we and others take in response to the words we speak or write.

ENCOURAGEMENT AND EDIFICATION

WHEN I WAS GROWING UP, my great-aunt Gillie McKinley was very influential in my life. Aunt Gillie's words were always uplifting. The Wisdom inside her guided her to impart hope to others through her words of encouragement. She made me feel ten feet tall and inspired me to dream big dreams.

In little accomplishments, Aunt Gillie saw the possibility of great things. She took the time to pleasantly and continually compliment me for small triumphs and to remind me that faithfulness in little things is the doorway to opportunities for achieving big dreams.

Oh, how we need Aunt Gillies in our lives today! Wisdom tells us that pleasant words like hers are like honey from a honeycomb, literally life to the soul and health to both the hearer and the giver. Pleasant words of encouragement positively affect our inside outlook, the way our physical body feels and our effectiveness and productivity.

Wisdom inside us gives wonderful graces that should be used to encourage and edify everyone with whom we have influence. Peace, gentleness and kindness inside manifest outwardly in caring, understanding, kind and supportive words that always encourage others. Aunt Gillie understood that encouragement is uplifting to both the giver and receiver.

Do you ever have days when it seems as if you are the cat on the porch that everybody kicks around? At those times, the best thing anyone could do for you would be to say something encouraging and uplifting. If we sow peaceable ways and words, we reap the fruits of graciousness. To have real friends, we have to show ourselves friendly first.

POWDER PUFF COMMUNICATION

WISDOM INSTRUCTS that a soft answer turns away anger but harsh words stir up anger and strife. The wise use knowledge wisely, but the mouth of a person who embraces and practices folly pours out foolishness. Wisdom also tells us that a wholesome tongue is a tree of life.

We communicate so many ways—through words, gestures and writing. Powder-puff communication is choosing soft words, a gentle manner, and considerate timing to express our honest thoughts and emotions. Our speech is a very powerful human capability, but words alone do not convey all meaning. Wisdom teaches us to be aware that our body language, facial expressions, tone of voice and other nonverbal communication must be "powder-puffed," in addition to our thoughts, emotions and words.

ELEPHANT EARS

It is the privilege of wisdom to listen.
—Oliver Wendell Holmes

Wisdom is very clear about the importance of listening to understand. Wisdom instructs us to be slow to speak and long, long, long on listening to hear and understand. Wisdom comes equipped with a room full of powder puffs and a big, big, big pair of elephant ears for listening—and hearing.

Have you ever listened without really hearing? Most likely, we all have done that at one time or another. Perhaps you have listened to your child prattle on about her day at kindergarten, not really paying attention, until she asks, "Was that okay for me to do that?"—and you realize you can't begin to answer because you never heard the question. Or perhaps a colleague came into your office with a concern, and you cut him off before he was finished speaking, giving him an answer to the question you *thought* he was going to ask. Or perhaps you have a friend who calls at an inconvenient time, and you keep doing what you were doing before the call, giving an occasional "uh-huh" to signal your presence, until a long pause in the conversation indicates that it's time for you to say something—and you don't know what to say because you haven't heard what your friend was saying to you.

Listening and hearing tells other people that you really care about them, their feelings and their thoughts. Harmonious, productive and lasting relationships are the result of empowering and enriching them by staying attuned to other people and responding wisely, serving them and meeting their expressed needs.

GOOD COMMUNICATION IS A HONED SKILL

WORDS DO HAVE POWER. Learning how to communicate is essential to making all of your vital relationships work. Success in any relationship depends on our making a conscious choice to listen and to hear. Then, when we have listened and heard, we can respond in a kind and gentle way, expressing love in our word choice, timing and manner of expression. After all, communication is not just the exchange of ideas or the transmission of information. It is also the expression of emotions and feelings. The old cliché "What you say is less important than how you say it" holds a lot of meaning! We should strive to improve our communication skills and then use them to communicate happily, responsibly, honestly and productively with everyone we meet or influence.

Folly leads us to believe that we can excuse ourselves from accountability and responsibility in communicating. This belief is wrong and terribly damaging. Wisdom is quite simple, quite straightforward about the necessity of following specific communication choices and skills:

1. We can choose to control our tongues and our written communication.
2. We can choose to speak and write only words that are constructive, kind, encouraging, forgiving, healing and respectful of and to everyone with whom we seek to communicate —regardless of the listener's gender, race, class, nationality or economic status. Wisdom even instructs us to communicate this way with those who might consider themselves our enemies.
3. We are to communicate the truth in love and avoid lecturing, preaching and self-righteousness.
4. We are never to give full vent to anger. Peace and forgiveness must be inherent in our communication, even if the topic of the conversation is unpleasant.
5. We must not use our great gift of speech for revenge.
6. We should avoid name-calling.
7. We should expect and accept in others what we also have— imperfections.
8. We are to pray for those with whom we are having conflicts and communication difficulties.
9. We must pray for change in ourselves more than for change in the other person.
10. We must always trust God to bring about necessary change in conditions, environment, circumstances and people. That means we don't take things into our own hands and don't manipulate.
11. We are to be on guard to forgive at all times, to look for openings and initiate them.
12. We must never hold a grudge.

And finally . . .
13. We must let our word be our bond.

Society rests on the integrity of every individual—and on promises being kept. In fact, broken promises can lead to the death of a society and the individual member, no matter how materially prosperous or skilled they may be.

My parents' word was their bond. When either or both made a promise, they made good on that promise regardless of circumstances or the actions of others. Nothing, absolutely nothing, would ever have justified in my father's mind, even the *thought* of being dishonorable. The pretty face of compromise was never pretty enough for my father to walk even close to the line. Dad would simply say, "When you play with fire, you get burned, and sometimes you get burned real, real bad. Dishonor, compromise and any strain of not keeping your word are what I mean by fire. Don't touch them, no matter how beautifully they glow." As Saint Paul taught—with few words and great Truth— *Let your yes mean yes, and your no mean no.*

This may seem like a daunting list of musts and shoulds, but it does take practice to make a habit of powder-puffed communication. The most important thing to remember about honing wise habits, such as good listening and speaking skills, is that we cannot rely on human strength alone or on philosophies of folly to get a good result, much less an excellent result. If we rely on Wisdom and the power of the Divine inside, then we can achieve excellent results in all our relationships.

NUGGET OF INSPIRATION

Two Important Words . . .
    Thank you
    We

        One Less Important Word . . .
    I

                . . . and Five Things to Remember
    Ruffle no feathers.
    Ban verbal assaults.
    No squawking.
    Silence is golden.
    Keep your promises.

PART THREE

Business Leadership HeartSkill

CHAPTER SIXTEEN

THE AVERAGE JOE

The first responsibility of a leader is to define reality. The last is to say thank you. In between the two, the leader must become a servant and a debtor . . . A friend of mine characterized leaders simply like this: "Leaders don't inflict pain; they bear pain."

—Max De Pree

REALITY CHECK

WISDOM. HONOR. HOPE. The Inner Path to True Greatness. Divine inspiration. Faith. Love. Truth. Peace . . .

What are these compared to the fiery, enticing glow of material wealth, prestige and instant gratification? You know—the "real" world. The real world where you "strike while the iron's hot," even if you "fry" the other guy or "burn some bridges" in the process. The real world that's ignited by short-term profits, hot looks and burning desires. Where success is touted if business is sizzling and the stock market is on fire. How can the Philosophy of Wisdom be part of this reality?

Well, in a way . . . it can't. As long as you view life through eyes that see this kind of existence as reality and truth, you will not be open to the Light that shimmers across your true path.

Until you distinguish what is "easily extinguished," you will not see what is truly enduring.

My father once asked me, "Son, do you remember the other night when we were camping and fishing and how quick those empty, dry pieces of wood burned, and how they popped and crackled as the wood disintegrated and the sparks disappeared into the night?"

I knew what he was referring to—in more ways than one. "Yes, Dad, I do," I answered. How well I also remember my life back in 1982 and how it went up in smoke, accompanied by lots of popping, crackling and sparks disintegrating into the night.

No, I didn't cheat or lie or steal. I didn't do anything that isn't routinely done in the business world every day. But I danced and dined with the compromise crowd. They seemed to have everything, but they really had nothing. Compromise was their name, folly was their game. And I had bought into the hand. As my dad pointed out, that dry wood on our camping trip, and my life without Wisdom, were unable to maintain themselves against stress. Emptiness was mostly what my choice's compromise had delivered to me. Through Dad's simple words, Wisdom delivered a wakeup call. I'm glad I answered, because I found a sure foundation for my life—a new reality—with an eternal outlook and an inner light of Wisdom, Honor and Hope.

You must *choose* to see a new reality—one where long-range goals, enduring values, ultimate peace, love and the Divine Presence create a clear picture of what life is all about. Does this mean you don't acknowledge what's happening around you, in your culture, in the world? Of course not! But you do not have to be part of the ways of the materialistic, frantic world as reality. Nope. You choose your MindSet. You choose your life. You choose your destiny. You choose your reality.

And yes, your chosen reality must extend to the workplace. You can't have one reality at home, at church and among friends, and then live by the business-world's other reality while at work. Well, actually, you can, but you'll get no real satisfaction, no real feeling of significance and no real benefit from such compromise—because you'll be reacting to a culturally-imposed reality *that's not real.* You, like the old me, will be left empty and unable to maintain against stress.

WHAT'S LEADING YOUR LIFE?

ASK YOURSELF:

- Do those who should be your focus take a backseat to your own selfish interests?
- Is your first priority to enrich yourself and your employer?
- Is the almighty profit dollar more important than treating others with fairness and respect?
- Do you excuse your behavior by denying responsibility for the consequences of your actions?

or . . .

- Do you use your talents, skills and abilities first to enrich the lives of your spouse, children, customers, peers and other people with whom you come in contact?
- When you make promises, do you keep them, no matter how insignificant they may seem, no matter what the circumstances?
- Do you treat everyone with dignity, regardless of their status in society?

. . . and the most important questions:

- Do your actions reflect the MindSet of Wisdom?
- Are you creating *lasting benefits* for yourself and for others whose lives you influence and impact each day?

Of course, you know by now that you don't want to be answering yes to those first four questions, right? Right!

If money or possessions are leading your life, you can't be a leader. If your emphasis on outward appearance is leading your life, you can't be a leader. If fear, shame, guilt or helplessness are leading your life, you cannot lead others. Only—and I will repeat—only if you are led by a spiritually open, wise heart can you lead others successfully.

Does this mean you'll make no mistakes? Nope. But you'll be led by enduring values and the HeartSkill and MindSet of

Wisdom that will equip you to make sound decisions and long-lasting meaningful plans. You'll be led to serve others, and in so doing, you will lead them.

Leaders who achieve lasting success follow these essential leadership principles of truth:

- They have disaffection for what is, passion for what can be.
- They seek first to understand, rather than to be understood.
- They use power and position to create opportunities for service.
- They elevate people and relationships above anything else.
- They serve graciously and humbly.
- They ask nicely, show appreciation and correct pleasantly.
- They give until it hurts, go the extra mile and forgive.
- Before deciding, they ask, "Is this best for all concerned?"

WHO ME?

I THINK I HEAR YOU . . . I think I hear you saying to yourself, "Hey, I can skip over this part. I'm not leadership material, anyway. I'm just an average Joe or Mary with a few strikes against me. But hey, I can work hard, and I can begin living from a spiritually minded viewpoint, and I can start to live by God's rules, but this leadership deal . . . I don't know . . . Me?

Yes, you. Once you're led by Divine influence, you radiate. I don't care if you are an average Joe, you will shine with some unearthly quality that employers and employees will notice and respect. The gracious goodness of Wisdom is magnetic, and you will be called upon to lead.

ANOTHER AVERAGE JOE

LET ME TELL YOU about another average Joe who ended up on the pages of history as a wise, industrious, and Divinely led leader. This wise leader was others-oriented in relationships with his peers, subordinates and all he affected on and off the job. He did not think he existed to be served, but rather, first and foremost, to serve and care for the needs of those within his sphere of influence. He adhered to his MindSet and viewpoint, despite the fact that the foolishness, downright cruelty and stupidity of others impacted his life.

Because Joe held Wisdom tight, even clung to it when others said that Wisdom was foolishness, Joe achieved excellence in all his roles and relationships—as son, brother, husband, father, friend, employee and leader.

Any one of us could be Joe. Joe truly was an average guy— not an intellectual giant, not born into royalty or great wealth. In fact, his family situation was a mite worse than dysfunctional—complete with jealous half-siblings and quarreling maternal figures—but he was his daddy's favorite son, and he was raised with wise teachings and spiritual values. But his brothers —raised with those same teachings—chose their own reality and assumed self-serving mindsets. They chose to despise Joe's favored status. Despite that, Joe loved his brothers and never wronged them in any manner.

There was something about him that was different. Wisdom inside motivated him to keep showing his brothers deep love because love makes up for others' faults. Genuine love continues to love even in unloving circumstances. They returned his love by plotting to kill him.

Focused on Joe's new coat and their own jealousies, they robbed him, took his clothes, threw him in an abandoned well and left him for dead. Then they left the scene of their crime and had a meal across the street. Okay . . . maybe his life was a bit worse than average!

While eating, these brothers noticed a group of merchants coming through town who looked very wealthy. Greedy for financial gain for themselves, the self-serving mindset led them to abort their plan to leave our average Joe to die. They approached the merchants and negotiated a sale. Joe became a slave of the merchants. And his shortsighted siblings received a few dollars for their efforts.

CORE OF INNER STRENGTH

BECAUSE HE HAD Wisdom inside, Joe maintained concentration on the big picture, filtered out the unimportant and fixed his thoughts on the good and the praiseworthy traits of his brothers. In his heart, he continued to be thankful for all his blessings. His mind and heart were filled with words and songs of praise.

Meanwhile, these self-serving brothers killed an animal and placed the animal's blood over Joe's clothing. With their deceitful plot in hand, they returned home. There they presented the clothing (their planted evidence) and told their father a cock-and-bull story about how Joe died.

The father believed them and grieved greatly. But he did not suspect his other sons. His trusting behavior showed Wisdom was inside him, too.

In the meantime, the slave master's self-serving mindset led him to turn a quick profit by flipping Joe to another slave master. You know what I mean, right? Like good, savvy business people do every day in today's modern marketplace where it is "more blessed to profit than it is to care."

This new master was more clever and smarter than the rogue siblings and the greedy merchant who first bought Joe. He too had a self-serving mindset, but he recognized a good value when he saw it. He saw how wise his slave Joe was by his manner of conduct and how he was able to make wise decisions.

To maximize his benefits, Joe's new owner placed the average Joe over his entire household and over all his many business enterprises. Joe's power and compensation became enormous because his results were astounding. And because of his relationship with Wisdom, his subordinates came to love this average Joe, who strove for excellence, not applause. This meant he served everyone, including his subordinates. They returned that love and there was nothing they wouldn't do for Joe. He didn't even have to ask.

WORSE THAN A VISIT TO THE DENTIST

ALONG COMES the master's wife. Talk about a self-serving mindset, now here was one that graded out at A+! She tempted ol' Joe to . . . well, you know what the temptation was! Being wise and a person of highest inner character and integrity he refused her advances. Wisdom inside was responsible for this behavior in a most difficult and trying moment. But when honor is the bedrock of our lives, that's the natural and habitual reaction of Wisdom.

What can I say? Naturally, she got really upset. So, upset at not getting her way, she ripped Joe's coat off as he ran out the door to escape. Afterward, in her self-serving mind, she stewed about not getting her desire and decided she could get revenge by manipulating the truth as well as her husband. She told her husband that the slave—that average Joe—tried to seduce her. Like the jealous siblings, she fabricated some evidence—again a coat.

You guessed it! The boss believed a lie from one with more power and influence than a slave.

Why? In his self-serving mindset, jumping to conclusions was natural. Truth and facts did not matter. Standing still long enough to think it through and get the facts was not part of his makeup. So, with this false perception firmly in mind, his boss punished Joe handsomely!

In one fell swoop Joe's inner character and integrity were "rewarded" by the loss of his job, his status, his income. Even worse, he was given a nice long prison sentence!

NUMB AND NUM'ER

BY NOW, SURELY you, the reader may be thinking "What a nightmare! This person has a dark cloud hanging over him. I surely don't want or need *his* methods and know-how. Right?"

But Joe continued to behave consistent with the Wisdom inside him. The MindSet of Wisdom flashed a message of Hope before his eyes that read: *Joe, this will be a great opportunity for you to grow.* Wisdom turned every loss into a greater gain.

In prison, the warden reached the same conclusion the prior slave master had, namely, That this average Joe was very wise and knew how to handle people and relationships very well. The warden, too, had the self-serving mindset. He decided to make a big return on no investment (free labor) and placed Joe over all the prisoners.

Our hero soon inherited what most would describe as a couple of numskull employees of the reigning king of that country. These peanut-heads had landed in prison because they had insulted the king.

Through the eyes of an understanding and a loving heart, Joe saw "Numb and Num'er" as unique, precious and valuable individuals and not two mismatched, unusable pieces of a worthless, dirty, tattered and torn old quilt. Numb and Num'er needed someone to understand their feelings, needed to feel needed, needed to be encouraged that they were not worthless because of their failures. Joe was "da man"!

Numb and Num'er kept having dreams and came to Joe for explanations, since he was obviously wise and spiritual. Joe listened and told Numb he would be out of prison in a few days, fully restored by the king to his former position. Then he told Num'er he would be hanged by the king within the same time frame. Even his kind heart could not sway his commitment to honesty.

Of course, Numb was so excited he didn't know whether to jump through the roof or kiss Joe's feet. Good ol' Joe told Numb he didn't owe a thing, but said it would be nice if he put in a good word for him with the king, since he was falsely imprisoned.

A few days later, the king had a feast and, sure enough, he had Num'er hanged and he fully restored Numb. You guessed it again! Numb forgot Joe's kindness. Numb's self-serving mindset landed him in prison the first time for being stupid, but being stupidly self-serving is not always cured by crisis. Numb figured this Joe guy was wise, but then again, he was in prison. So Numb figured he'd learn nothing by observing Joe's MindSet of Wisdom. And he didn't.

Patience, Joe. . . .

Two years passed. The king had a recurring dream, over and over, night after night. He called together all the wise people in his kingdom and asked them to interpret his dreams. None could.

Numb finally remembered his promise. Actually, Numb saw the opportunity to do something for the king that could mean big rewards for Numb. See, Numb still did not have the HeartSkill of Wisdom, he still operated from the self-serving mindset that had once landed him in prison.

Numb told the king about the average Joe, the king's imprisoned slave, and of course, the king quickly issued a summons. He verbally put this nobody up on the pedestal, stroking his released prisoner's ego about how wise he had heard he was. Of course, our average Joe remained quite humble, avoiding bitterness and asserting that his ability to listen to and interpret dreams came from a Divine source. The king could have locked him up again after that comment, but Joe undoubtedly displayed a charismatic and inspired confidence and humility.

Joe did interpret the king's dreams. He told the king how the kingdom would have seven years of prosperity followed by seven years of famine. And naturally Joe showed genuine concern for those who would be affected by the famine.

THOUGHTFULNESS vs. INTELLECT AND CLEVERNESS

WISDOM INSIDE taught Joe that love comes before knowledge and self-serving interests. That same Wisdom moved him to look beyond selfish gain. He refused to keep Wisdom bottled up, and instead chose to use it to help others, despite the fact that no financial or other reward was offered.

So he shared with the king how to prepare and plan for the famine by saving and storing up in the years of plenty. The king liked the plan and proclaimed the wisdom of Joe's interpretation and plan. He asked his most trusted advisers whom they would recommend to oversee the plan's execution. (The self-serving mindset makes us blind in our power and expertise to the obvious that novices see).

Unfortunately, the king's advisers could think of no one that wise or disciplined enough to stick with a plan that called for sacrifice in times of plenty. They knew most people would waste and abuse power in times of plenty. But our humble hero remained quiet—and did not despair.

ANYTHING YOU DREAM IS POSSIBLE

GUIDED BY WISDOM, an expert knows he must always consider good counsel, regardless of the source. Nudged by the Spirit of God to consider Joe, the king appointed him. Here's where Joe's Wisdom paid off! With much public fanfare, the king not only proclaimed to all in his kingdom that Joe was to be in charge of overseeing the plan but he also had him made second-in-command over an entire nation! With the honor came privileges and rewards like a new title, a new wardrobe, a new vehicle, an entourage of people waiting on him hand and foot and a beautiful princess as a wife. In addition to all of that, the king gave Joe power of attorney, making his word or signature as good as the king's.

Our average Joe—the king's right-hand man—was only thirty years old when the king appointed him. (I didn't mention age deliberately. Wisdom and the MindSet of Wisdom are not age exclusive. Remember Numb? Apparently he never got it, regardless of how much older he became.)

During the seven years of plenty, Joe, now the leader, fulfilled his responsibility with integrity. His new family flourished because he made them a priority over work. On the job, he neither abused his position or power nor compromised his Wisdom-based beliefs, principles, values or priorities to chase philosophies of humanism, materialism, intellectualism or hedonism.

PRECIOUS INNER STONES: WISDOM, HONOR AND HOPE

BECAUSE OF JOE's FIDELITY to Wisdom, the resources that he had to work with were multiplied far beyond his hopes. So much so that even he stopped measuring and trying to keep up with how much was being stored for the years of famine.

By now, I guess we can't really call him average anymore . . .

Joe has risen to the top, as it were, but it was certainly not through luck, birthright or privilege. It was because he never wavered from his real job in life—to serve when needed, to console or teach when needed, to work with honor. He lived with the MindSet of Wisdom, followed its others-first caregiving strategy to a T and ultimately reaped the rewards.

When famine struck the king's nation, Joe and his crew had done their job—and then some! Not only had Joe provided for all the local citizens to eat and live comfortably, but he was also able to open the storehouses of food and other items to sell—at very fair, uninflated prices—to affected outlying nations. He graciously considered the welfare of others over selfish financial gain.

Joe's elderly, loving father and misguided rogue siblings were also radically impacted by the famine. His father heard about what this planning commissioner in another nation had done, and he sent the brothers to buy grain from him, not knowing that he was sending them to the brother they had wronged.

But here is where Wisdom's amazing disposition really shows through. Joe was gracious and did business with his long-lost brothers (who failed to recognize him)! When conditions got worse for Joe's father and the rogue siblings, they sought to move to this nation of plenty. Joe went to bat for them with the king and finally told them that he was their kid brother whom they had sold so long ago—and that he forgave them. Joe treated them as if they had never wronged him; he loved them unconditionally.

Because of Joe's high position in the eyes of the king and the Wisdom, Honor and Hope that Joe had brought to his new nation, the king gave the rogue siblings and the overjoyed father some choice land to live on and positions that assured them of living abundantly. Even when Joe's father died—and his brothers feared revenge—Joe and his brothers continued to live in harmony, abundantly and contentedly, for many years. Joe humbly and willingly continued as a "slave" in charge of the king's nation and his legacy endures to this day—as the wise Joseph of Egypt in the book of Genesis, chapters 37 through 50. It's worth looking it up, to refresh your memory.

TOUCH THE SKY

THE AVERAGE JOE can be a mighty leader by serving always. The average Joe can live with greatness by attending to the small things that matter. The average Joe can make his life mean something just by believing that it already does mean something. The average Joe . . . can be you.

NUGGET OF INSPIRATION

Each of us can be great . . . because each of us can serve. A college degree is not required to serve. We only need a heart full of grace, a soul generated by love.
—(personal paraphrase of) Reverend Dr. Martin Luther King Jr.

CHAPTER SEVENTEEN

GETTING DOWN TO BUSINESS

There's a way to do it better—Find it.
—Thomas A. Edison

There is always a best way of doing everything.
—Ralph Waldo Emerson

THE HEARTSKILL AND MINDSET OF WISDOM ARE THE KEY INGREDIENTS TO BUSINESS SUCCESS

INDIVIDUALS MAY have two mindsets in their approach to personal and business roles and relationships. One is the self-serving mindset, which is selfish in choices and actions. The other is the HeartSkill and MindSet of Wisdom, which put others first in choices and actions. We have seen how the HeartSkill and MindSet of Wisdom enhance individual lives and personal relationships. Now let's look at how they affect business roles and relationships.

Having been a businessman myself for many years, I approach Wisdom in business from the perspective of business leadership. But the principles apply to everyone who works in the business world at every level of responsibility. Everything in

171

this chapter is equally applicable to families and to all personal roles and relationships. I challenge you to consider the following points:

You are a leader.

When you run your life by the Philosophy of Wisdom and create a life of significance, you assume a position of leadership. This may not mean you hold a job with that title, but the very nature of the Spirit-led life is influential—and your example, your decisions, your habits and the gracious goodness of Wisdom *will* influence others. Therefore, you are asked to humbly accept the title and the servitude it demands.

You run a business.

It is part of our human nature to produce, create, nurture, discover, build, analyze, synthesize, ponder, express, assist and labor. You probably won't do the same kind of work all your life, but there is one job description that will always describe you: You'll always be "you" for a living. That's right. You are [*fill in your own name here*] for a living—no matter what trade you pursue, no matter who your employer may be or whom you employ. If you are the president of a large company, the manager of a retail store, the file clerk in the front office or a blueberry farmer—you are [*fill in your own name here*] for a living. Therefore, your approach to any work you do is important, isn't it?

In fact, you're basically the president—the leader—of your own one-man or one-woman company and anyone who ever pays you is one of your clients. If you bag groceries, the grocer is your client and you owe him the best that your one-person company can offer. You may not remain in that particular line—you may then go on to selling real estate or running the advertising department of a traveling rodeo show—but you'll still be the president of the company that offers *you* as the asset and worker, even though your principal client changes. Strange concept? Maybe. But change your MindSet and you'll take a whole new gander at how you see yourself as an employee if you answer to yourself and your standards. And if you're walking with

God to create a meaningful and significant life, then you're not just answering to yourself . . . are you?

Humphry Osmond said that there is no one else who can ever fill your role in the same way, so it's a good idea to perform it as well as possible. Think on that. Then believe it and start seeing yourself as "running your own business" even if you're in a cubicle surrounded by fifty-two other folks in their own cubicles "running their own businesses." Run your business—your work—with the same Wisdom-based MindSet that you run your personal life and you'll be headed down the path of success.

A CAUTIONARY NOTE!

I'M NOT SUGGESTING that you run out and literally become self-employed by starting your own business! Being responsible for every facet of a business is skilled work in and of itself, and may not fit with your talents or dreams. Being your own boss in the legal sense may sound exciting, but do you have the right perception of and attitude about what you must do to make a business successful and keep it that way? Let me challenge you to be honest with yourself about a few essential facts.

- Are you ready to commit to long hours?
- Are you self-disciplined and a self-starter?
- Can you work without the security of a steady paycheck?

Consider these questions carefully and honestly before you start a business. The lure of being your own boss, having the freedom to do what you want, when you want, are thoughts that you might want to check at the door. When choosing for yourself, do not deceive yourself. Instead, act according to Wisdom's laws and principles, and you will make the right choice for yourself, your family and everyone else involved.

DOES A BUSINESS HAVE A SOUL?

WELL, NOT REALLY, but we can look at a business and its leadership and determine if it is on the right path—if it is linked with Divine purpose. In fact, businesses flounder or fail for the same reasons that people don't achieve their potential. And a business can flourish, influence and profit in the same way that an individual can attain harmony in life and true greatness. This English proverb applies to the individual as well as those who run a business: Consider well who you are, what you do, whence you came, and whither you are to go.

WHY DO MANY NEW BUSINESSES FAIL?

THERE ARE FIVE primary reasons why businesses fail.

1
LACK OF A WRITTEN BUSINESS PLAN

This is one of the most common reasons new businesses fail. In fact, many of the other pitfalls relate directly to the lack of a written business plan. Just like a personal financial plan, a written business plan can help you plan your destination. If you have a well-written plan, you will be more likely to arrive at success in your business. The best business plans keep you focused on your long-term goals. A business plan can be a tool to force you, initially and during the normal course of business, to apply Wisdom's laws and principles.

2
IMPROPER CAPITALIZATION

Wisdom's principles are especially critical to the way in which you initially capitalize your business, affecting the amounts, types and sources of your business capital. Equity capital (which involves payment to a business of money in exchange for ownership or profit participation) is preferable to debt capital. This opinion is based on financial rationale, as well as the spiritual aspects of borrowing money. Wisdom clearly teaches us that borrowing money (debt capitalization) is less desirable from a spiritual point of view than raising equity capital (investment).

3
FAILURE TO MEASURE SUCCESS THE RIGHT WAY

Measure quantitative success by cash flow, not by sales. Sales and sales growth are important, but neither necessarily translates into profits, cash flow or capital that can fund either distributions to the owner(s) or future growth. Count sales and receivables only when the money has been collected.

4
SKILL DEFICIENCIES

The skills necessary to conceive a business, to finance start-up and to get everything off the ground are not the same as the leadership, management and labor skills required to keep the business going or expand it. If you start a business or own one now, you may need additional training and education yourself. You may need to hire competent help. Be prudent in hiring: some jobs are so important that the person you hire needs to have proven skills. As my dad would say, "You always get what you pay for, and most of the time, if you have used Wisdom, you get what you thought you paid for."

5
MISPERCEPTION

The seven myths of business are another classic example of how false perception occurs when the traditionally held viewpoint is accepted without the search for or consideration of the Truth. Many people in the workplace believe the following seven myths about businesses or other organizations:

Myth 1. It takes a great idea to succeed.
Myth 2. Leaders must be charismatic.
Myth 3. The foremost priority is to maximize profit.
Myth 4. The best decisions result from planning.
Myth 5. Vision *alone* leads to success.
Myth 6. Personal and business values do not mix.
Myth 7. Working by Wisdom's values reduces profit.

Because these are false perceptions, they frequently are the source of very bad decisions. My advice? Learn and apply the Philosophy of Wisdom's system of thinking. Don't be victimized by any or all of these myths. Pursue your dreams skillfully. Possess and apply the HeartSkill of Wisdom.

Wisdom's system of thinking can be used to discern Truth, cause us to choose and act wisely and help us not to be victims of false perceptions.

THE DANGER OF LEVERAGED AMBITION—
THE DEBT TRAP

WHETHER YOU OWN your own business, work in a support position for a small company or are appointed chief financial officer of a large computer-chip manufacturer, you are at some level responsible for money—your own paycheck or the financial health of your client, the company! The first rule to follow with matters of money is to beware of credit!

Credit of all types allows us individually and in business to avoid the pain of discipline, to take what seems to be the easy way and thumb our noses at prudence. Credit also appeals to excessive appetites. It panders to the desire to have what we want and have it today. The use of credit in business may begin innocently enough. But eventually, we lose the ability to distinguish between wants and needs. Wants may even *become* needs, and frequently, the only way to meet our desires is to rob from tomorrow's or next year's income. So we borrow. Easy credit becomes a slave master in business. We discover there are too many expenses for our business's bank account and those so-called easy payments get tough.

Debt is dangerous. It presumes on tomorrow and makes us vulnerable to compromise. Wisdom does not say that debt should never be used. Wisdom does instruct us clearly against overindulgence. Wisdom also teaches that those who embrace and apply Wisdom should remain or become debt free, so that they are in a position to lend, interest free, to others. Wisdom instructs that debt should not be used to finance expansion for expansion's sake, and that we should be prudent and use discretion with debt.

Living within boundaries is the only way to attain the highest, lasting success in personal or business life.

Use debt sparingly, and be sure that your desires and motives align with Wisdom's.

Better yet, be a lender who does not charge interest; give away a percentage of every dollar of profit to truly needy persons such as widows and orphans; and give jobs to the economically disadvantaged.

HOW WISDOM-BASED BUSINESSES SUCCEED!

THERE ARE SEVEN key ingredients of lasting business success in a Wisdom-based business:

Key 1. Enduring purpose and vision
Key 2. Unity
Key 3. Commitment to mission
Key 4. Effective communication
Key 5. Need-based services and products
Key 6. Sound capitalization
Key 7. Sound preparation, planning, systems and processes

In the real world, these key ingredients boil down to the beliefs, truths, principles, values and priorities of leaders. Leaders have the power to establish business philosophy (the conceptual way they believe the business should operate) and how that philosophy is practiced in day-to-day operations.

Business leadership and management involve things like plans, budgets, time, conflict, innovation and ideas. Lasting success (achieving enduring purpose) in business, however, depends on wise leadership of people and wise management of vital business relationships.

In the absence of a truly enduring purpose and vision, the other key ingredients to lasting business success cannot be of highest quality. Enduring purpose and vision can only exist when the leaders' philosophy is founded on highest beliefs, principles and values, namely Wisdom.

The core beliefs, principles and values of those in leadership are imputed to the organization. These, not leadership's vision or intellectual and moral ideals, establish the organization's true purpose and determine the degree of unity and commitment in the organization.

PURPOSE, VISION, AND MISSION

LEADERS SHOULD always begin their business preparation and planning by defining purpose, casting a vision of the results and determining the mission of the business.

Purpose

PURPOSE IS the reason for which something exists or is made or done. It can refer to the entire business to some specific segment or activity within the business. Purpose describes the end we want to achieve and the starting point that determines everything we do and why everything exists. A business should place high value on its purpose. Without purpose, the activities we engage in lose relevance and generally end in failure. And since purpose is the reason for existence or action, the purpose of the business is the overarching accomplishment the business is focused on attaining. The purpose is a direct result of core beliefs, principles and values.

Purpose results from beliefs and principles, and beliefs and principles are held by people. To set a course, leaders must have a reason for making the journey. The first step in defining the purpose of the business is defining the core beliefs, principles and values of the leaders of the business. These are imputed to the business and become the foundation of its character.

In the pages of Wisdom, Jesus taught that there are two ways a house can be built, on rock or on sand. The house built on rock endures through all the storms, but a house built on sand will be washed away. This story is also meaningful in evaluating the purpose for which a business is built. If the purpose of a business is based on Wisdom's core beliefs, principles and values, then the purpose will be enduring and the business will have a strong foundation. Wisdom-based leadership prepares, plans and operates the business on Wisdom's core principles, beliefs and values. A business foundation and operating approach based on Wisdom ensure that a business will remain strong enough to weather frequent storms.

Profit is important, and I am definitely a strong advocate of the capitalist approach to business and profits. The chief aim of a business guided by the Philosophy of Wisdom, however, is serving God by serving others.

As Adam Smith taught, profit is not the end for a business, it is the reward a business receives from serving the general welfare.

Vision-Casting

WISDOM INSTRUCTS that where there is no vision, the people perish. Leaders must set new goals as previous ones are attained. New goals are the fuel of forward momentum. With Wisdom and the Spirit of God inside us, nothing is impossible in leadership, in business or in our lives! The starting point for profitable ideas is to figure out what others really need and then to truly want to help them get it. This is business operating in harmony with Wisdom's principles and values.

Once purpose has been established, leaders must develop a mental picture of what the purpose will look like when it has been achieved. This is vision-casting. Vision-casting is significantly enhanced by the highest HeartSkill of Wisdom. It is the bridge from beliefs, truths and principles to actions. Vision-casting allows leaders to communicate the vision and clearly define tasks to employees so that they can understand what the eventual results will yield for them—as well as for customers, vendors, other third parties, the leaders and the business itself. This is helpful in reducing the anxiety and fear that can sap productivity.

Vision, resulting from a wise purpose, can motivate employees to act in a manner that will achieve the purpose. A clear view of the end, established from an enduring purpose, establishes unity within a business. Recasting the vision of a business is a first step in changing a business's poor past results into excellent future results.

Mission

ONCE LEADERS HAVE defined a business purpose and cast a vision of the results, they must establish the mission of the business. Mission is a function of the enduring purpose and the vision. *Purpose* is the effect leadership wants the business to achieve, *vision* is what leadership thinks the effect will look like, and *mission* is what will cause the desired result to be realized. Therefore, business mission is also a function of the core beliefs, principles and values imputed by leadership to the business. A sound and well-developed business mission leads to the third key ingredient, commitment to mission. When employees have high confidence in the actions for achieving the desired results, they will be committed to carrying out those actions.

EFFECTIVE COMMUNICATION

THE FOURTH KEY INGREDIENT to lasting business success is effective communication. In all communication, the objective should be understanding—that is, knowledge comprehended well enough to be used for productive purpose. If you doubt the importance of understanding as the objective of all communication, then consider an Old Testament story. God wanted to break the unity and commitment of the workers building the Tower of Babel because their motive was wrong. They wanted to become independent of God. What method did God use? He introduced a language barrier, effectively ending all productive communication among the builders of the tower. No communication, no understanding—no tower!

There are two keys to effective communication.

1
SKILLFULLY LISTENING TO THE OTHER PERSON
OR PERSONS IN THE COMMUNICATION LINK

Listen carefully for the other person's intended meaning. Pay attention to tone of voice, timing and body language. Careless listening can cause misperception of intended meaning and unwise thinking that leads to unwise decisions.

2
WHEN YOU SPEAK OR WRITE, FOLLOW THE KISS
SYSTEM—KEEP IT SIMPLE, STUPID

Think before you speak or write anything. Be sure you understand what your intended meaning is.

Consider whether now, later or perhaps never is the right time to express yourself. Timing matters!

If you decide to express yourself, choose your words, tone and body language with care. Then practice your message in your mind. Express your thoughts and feelings by using a wise tone of voice. Be sure your body language conveys your intended meaning clearly and accurately.

Listen skillfully to the response of the person to whom you are communicating. Make sure your message was received and understood.

HONOR PRECEDES PUBLIC TRUST—
DELIVER THE GOODS

INTEGRITY IS CRUCIAL in communication. Customer communication needs to state facts honestly, with a gracious attitude. When marketers do not represent a product or service truthfully and graciously, customers become alienated from the buying process. Inaccurate or downright dishonest information or aggressive attitudes will cause customers to mistrust a business. That is why it is so important for marketing, sales and customer relations communication and interactions to agree with Wisdom's core beliefs, principles and values.

In all marketing, sales and customer relations communication and interaction:

- Use the same words consistently and explain those words thoroughly when you first use them.
- Be sure that verbal and nonverbal communications are consistent with each other, as well as with the purpose, vision and mission of the business.
- Repeat key items to make sure they are understood and that the audience understands their importance.
- Establish feedback. Observe the effect of your message on your audience or potential customers. Did they receive the message with the same intent with which you sent the message?
- Understand the attitudes, backgrounds and beliefs of your audience or potential customers, and be sure that you take them into account when preparing your message.
- Establish clear, precise, and measurable goals that you want your message to accomplish over a specific time.

Marketing, sales and customer relations communication and interaction must be designed and executed in ways that influence the customer to make an initial transaction and repeat transactions with the business. In your marketing, sales and customer relations communication, say what you mean and mean what you say, and do both graciously.

NEED-BASED SERVICES AND PRODUCTS

LET'S LOOK AT TWO examples of how products were developed based on broad-based needs, rather than on expressed customer needs and wants.

Most people at the end of the nineteenth century thought the horseless carriage was a pipe dream. Obviously then, the automobile was not developed in response to market demand (a large group of customers did not express a need or want for an automobile). The automobile was developed because visionaries who understood the power of customer beliefs and values perceived that the public had a desire to get from point A to point B quickly. The need or want was the conservation of time, and the automobile provided a partial solution to that need or want. In this case, you might surmise that the automobile created a market, but that is not exactly what happened.

The automobile satisfied an unexpressed need or want that was present in individuals. *Unexpressed needs and wants,* seen in the mind's eye of a visionary leader, created the automobile market. Eventually, the automotive industry grew to the point where today it accounts for approximately one of every six manufacturing jobs in the United States.

In another example, the personal computer was not developed because there was a market for them or because a large group of customers had expressed a need or want for a home or small-business computer. Most people assumed computers were limited to applications in large organizations where the financial and space resources were available to accommodate the existing technology. The nonmainframe-computer revolution began in businesses as a method of providing greater flexibility.

As more people became familiar with computer use in their businesses, a few visionaries saw the ability for these products to satisfy needs in personal lives. Today, more than 40 percent of

U.S. households have a personal computer. The transition was so quick that the leaders of many large computer manufacturers missed the boat. They either exited the market too early or spent vast sums to catch up.

The lesson to be learned from these two examples is the power of customer beliefs and values and the importance of thinking like a customer—not that products or services establish needs and wants. Once a product or service is developed by a visionary to satisfy a customer's need or want, then customers will respond. Businesses and business leaders that focus on customer beliefs, values, needs and wants will continually achieve superior results.

SOUND CAPITALIZATION

APPLICATION OF WISDOM's laws and principles is especially critical to how you initially choose the amounts, types and sources of capital for your business. When you project your capital needs, focus on worst-case scenarios. Be very hard on your expectations of success, considering things such as unexpected and significant delays in opening, or greater competition. Figure on high operating overhead and low sales, then add an additional cushion to cover anything you may have overlooked. Do not use your best-case scenarios or even your good or average scenarios to make your final decision about the amount of capital you will initially need to capitalize your business. It is better to be safe than sorry. Be as sure as you can that you have planned and capitalized in a way that guards against running out of money before you establish your business in the marketplace. And, as I mentioned before, remember that equity (invested) capital is preferable to debt capital from a business standpoint and from a spiritual standpoint.

REJECT THE FIRE DRILL MENTALITY

MANY, MANY PERSONAL and business families are like fire drills: run here, run there, put out this fire and move to the next. This happens when leaders ignore preparation and planning.

The servant attitude of the MindSet of Wisdom is based on love, and there is no fear in love. So the servant attitude works to eliminate fear. Preparation greatly reduces uncertainty. In return, uncertainty significantly reduces fear, distress and anxiety. Most of us can relate to this scenario from our school days. Did you ever neglect or forget to study for a test? Remember how you felt when you entered the classroom and took your seat? You probably suffered fear, anxiety and distress as a result of your lack of preparation.

A leader who has a spiritually wise heart and a servant attitude views preparation as a critically important activity.

- Preparation reduces fear.
- Preparation reduces the chance of failure.
- Preparation allows people to increase their level of achievement, and this in turn reduces the chance for failure.
- Preparation increases confidence, and confidence significantly reduces fear.

Preparation, therefore, is an integral part of the servant attitude because to serve means to give, and to give means to improve, and to improve means to make better.

NUGGET OF INSPIRATION

As you enter positions of trust and power, dream a little before you think.

—Toni Morrison

CHAPTER EIGHTEEN

KILLER ATTITUDES

Make money. Have fun. Be ethical. These are the three keys to a successful business career, given to me years ago by my boss. I've repeated them to everybody I've ever hired. Sometimes an eyebrow will go up. Ethics? Some people don't think of that as a necessary part of a first-day briefing. It's not in their frame of reference. And that's exactly what the problem is.

—Don Peppers

WHO YOU ARE IN BUSINESS . . . IS WHO YOU ARE. PERIOD.

THE PITFALLS of non-Wisdom-based decisions and behaviors in the world of business are everywhere, unfortunately. Even persons who are *resolved* to live spiritually within the business environment can find themselves succumbing to rationale and attitudes that thwart not only personal happiness but the health and success of the business—and eventually the bottom line.

Plato said that right behavior results from the harmony and control of reason, passion and appetite. Harmony, with ourselves or others, is impossible when we follow decision-making models that are self-focused in beliefs, principles and values. Attitudes are a clear outward indicator of our inner spirit-person's character and integrity. Attitudes demonstrate the state of affairs inside us, what qualities our inner spirit-person really harbors, and what we are predisposed to do.

Unwise and destructive leadership attitudes and behaviors create all sorts of problems when manifested by anyone within a personal or business family, but especially when leaders exemplify them. Selfish perception often centers its attention on material possessions that may be seen, handled and owned. Insincere words or actions indicate lack of character and integrity. Silence and inaction in the face of injustice show a lack of honesty and compassion. All these unwise attitudes draw our attention away from what really matters from an eternal perspective. Leaders' attitudes affect other people, and their choices bear consequences for everyone with whom they have a personal or business relationship.

TURN 'EM LOOSE

WE HUMANS HAVE developed psychology and philosophy to help deal with our attitudes and emotions. Much value has been provided and much good accomplished through the efforts of competent professionals in these disciplines. Self-control, for example, is a technique taught in both psychology and philosophy. Both teach that we can control overactive feelings. But psychology and philosophy are inherently faulty as systems upon which to base our lives, because they both rely on human capabilities and human strengths and they both ignore questions of eternal significance.

We can achieve harmony only with Wisdom inside, relying on the strength of the Divine within to help us make wise choices. Wisdom teaches that every choice we make has eternal consequences. It just makes sense to rely on the best system available for guidance in making those choices, and that is Wisdom. Wisdom's way is better, more powerful and eminently more able to deliver truly durable benefits for us and those in relationships with us. Wisdom is the only way to break out of killer attitudes and move on positively and successfully. It took the return to Wisdom for me to change my self-serving mindset and place my feet once again firmly on the Inner Path to True Greatness.

I have already revealed some of the undesirable leadership attitudes and behavior that dominated my life for fifteen years, so you know that I have personal and painful experience with the unwise leadership attitudes and behaviors that I am trying my best to help you steer clear of, with Wisdom's solution. With Wisdom, you can overcome attitudes that are shallow, manipulative, arrogant and excessively proud, clever and sarcastic, pretentious, and obsessive.

UNPRODUCTIVE ATTITUDES

Shallowness

SHALLOWNESS IS THE SOURCE of great difficulties and conflicts in relationships. Rather than engage in any deep thought when considering a different viewpoint on a topic, many of us find it much easier to construct a rational, well-argued case for whatever point of view we already hold. We become the prisoners of our views, simply because we can coherently articulate and staunchly defend our positions, whether or not they are wise positions. Some of us have become so capable of defending our point of view that even questioning or exploring the subject matter further seem to be a waste of time. From my experience and observation, when people think they are right and can demonstrate that to others, communication is over before it begins. The result of shallowness is stalemate as leaders and followers both come to believe that it is unnecessary to listen to another view.

A wise leader seeks to solve problems and increase productivity and efficiency by serving others and tapping into their vast reservoirs of innovative and creative ability. The most expensive, least efficient and unproductive ways of doing anything are summarized in the following expressions, which are echoed far too often in the halls and hearts of business leaders:

1. We've always done it this way.
2. This will never work.
3. The best way to get ahead is not to rock the boat.

These express shallow leadership attitudes that kill creativity, promote inefficiency, stifle communication and put lids on productivity.

Manipulation

MANIPULATION IS YET another unwise outgrowth of the self-serving mindset. Our inner character vices, virtues and graces are products of our belief system. When our belief system is based on the self-serving mindset, a model for thinking that is self-focused, vices such as manipulation are prevalent and graces are often nonexistent. Many people manipulate others in their personal and business roles and relationships. I know. I've been there and done that—and I deeply regret it.

Manipulation is rooted in pride and selfishness, and treats other people as objects. Its driving need to control can manifest as compulsive controlling behavior. Manipulators use their knowledge, power or position to limit the freedom of others and to exercise control over them by using tools such as deceit and distortion. Manipulation is destructive to the manipulator and to those who are manipulated. It often buys a lot of relationship heartache, sorrow, grief and destruction.

On the other hand, true concern for others' best interests moves us to act according to Wisdom's motive and passion. Unconditional love supports and releases. The desire to serve others leads us toward wise action. Wisdom's inner character graces steer us away from manipulation in our roles and relationships.

Mercy and grace are choices. Wise choices to forgive and forget are keys to conflict resolution that keep relationships intact. Grace and mercy set one free from the selfish traps of bitterness, unforgiveness and other killer attitudes.

Arrogance and Excessive Pride

ARROGANCE AND EXCESSIVE PRIDE create artificial distinctions in our minds between ourselves and others. We want to think that others are different from us in some way, so we create artificial distinctions and act on them in a self-serving way. Such artificial distinctions affect our emotions and, thus, our personal and business decisions. Arrogance and excessive pride block our ability to be sensitive toward others. Instead of being empathetic, we cannot recognize and appreciate the reality of others' situations. Thus it is not possible for us to be truly others-oriented in critical personal and business relationships. This endangers the integrity of these relationships and threatens their very existence.

Clever and Sarcastic Wit

PLACING A HIGH VALUE on cleverness and sarcastic wit can also result from the self-serving mindset. These were two of my most prominent mental attitudes from 1967 to 1981. I must still combat these two attitudes every day, relying on Truth and the Spirit of God within me for the power to defeat them.

Many people prefer cleverness and sarcasm over insightful thinking and sensitivity to others because of the immediate reinforcement it offers—a feeling of superiority. This superior feeling is yet another unwise attitude, with no basis in reality. Cleverness and sarcasm lack soundness and depth. Yet, as I did for far too long, many people rely on them in their personal and business roles, relationships and decision making. We can become really puffed up about our own self-importance when we perceive we have proven someone else wrong or attacked their self-worth.

Cleverness and sarcasm are usually expressions of excessive pride or of hidden feelings of inferiority that radically and negatively affect the quality of our thinking, our choices and our actions. That is why cleverness and sarcasm can be significant barriers to achieving truly enduring success in our roles and relationships.

Pretension

I WAS AMAZED at the results of a recent national poll about casual dress in the workplace. Some prominent leaders expressed concern about workers wearing casual attire in the workplace. They thought followers would lose respect for leaders. What are we coming to when we believe that real respect for leadership is based on suits, ties and button-down collars? *Leadership pretension* is just another barrier to best results.

We need to let down the superficial barriers that separate us from others. What's in the heart is what really counts. What *is* the proper clothing for leaders? Wisdom instructs us to clothe leadership in humility.

Some of us, in order to belong, engage in what I call *economic pretension*. This was one of my favorite activities from 1967 to 1981. Sometimes economic pretension is called keeping up with the Joneses—a useless waste of time, energy and resources if there ever was one. Motivational speaker Charlie Jones once said, "Just about the time you catch up with the Joneses, they refinance and go on yet another spending, pretending binge."

We engage in economic pretension so that others will affirm our value. We seek approval from strangers, as well as from people we know, based on the clothes we wear, the neighborhood we live in, the car we drive or the school we attended. Economic pretension has a huge impact on decisions and behavior in our personal and business roles and relationships.

A third form of pretension is *relationship pretension*. This is better known as hypocrisy. We pretend we are living according to understood relationship standards, when in fact we are not. Many people either compromise their spiritual beliefs and values or exclude them altogether in their roles and relationships.

A fourth form of pretension is *intellectual pride*. This too was one of my biggest weaknesses from 1967 to 1981 because of the self-serving mindset I had. This form of pretension involves pretending superiority over others based on having a higher IQ, more advanced academic degrees or excessive cleverness. Humans often value such differences far too highly. We place too much value on intellectual prowess and cleverness and not enough on serving others and appreciating others' gifts.

But we can choose to reject leadership, economic and relationship pretension and intellectual pride by developing true inner integrity founded on Wisdom's core spiritual beliefs and values.

Obsession

AN OBSESSION IS an emotionally charged idea that repetitively and insistently invades our consciousness. Sometimes an obsession is welcomed, whereas at other times we do our best to block it out but cannot. Obsessions frequently indicate serious underlying problems. They can become pervasive and dangerous when they interfere with our ability to think and behave rationally in personal and business roles and relationships.

Eventually, inward obsessions manifest outwardly as compulsive behavior that can end in role and relationship disaster. Compulsive behavior includes destructive use of the tongue and destructive acts, such as attacking others and excessive spending, especially when the currency is credit. Often quarrels with and attacks on others, and spending sprees, are a means to other ends: the passion for recognition and status, revenge, spite for a perceived slight or a soothing salve for the conscience.

Wisdom can help us avoid these attitudes and conflicts. Wisdom and Truth inside us birth the inner graces, and the outward personality expressions of graciousness, humility, justice and compassion. The principles and values of Wisdom and the Spirit of God within ensure that we will ask ourselves every day, *What pride of mine is standing in the way of some good I can do today?*

Anyone who has a distorted notion of his or her own importance is probably seeing through one or more unwise attitudes. When we see through these, we misperceive the true purpose of our lives, namely, to serve God and others.

The HeartSkill and MindSet of Wisdom, and the gracious goodness of Wisdom's amazing disposition are the permanent solutions for these and all other unwise attitudes. Wisdom's amazing disposition cannot be faked and is only possible when our outward personality reflects a Wisdom-based inner character and integrity.

MOVING AWAY FROM DIVISIVE CONFLICT

INTERNAL DIVISION HAS A GREATER negative impact on profitability than external factors like competition or inflation. No matter how highly educated, experienced, intellectually or physically gifted a person may be, if their core beliefs, principles and values are not consistent with Wisdom's, that person is a candidate to eventually be a source for division. Division is the opposite of unity; unity is the foundation upon which commitment to mission can be built.

Can conflict ever be good and positive for individuals and organizations? Yes, conflict can be the source of character growth, and it can be an impetus for needed change. Differing opinions are often what help us understand our own opinions and keep reexaming them. Differing opinions can also help us avoid pursuit of what the test of time would prove to be unwise or harmful beliefs, perceptions or related actions.

Leaders who desire the highest lasting success for themselves and their families or businesses will act to prevent divisive conflict and develop and maintain a wise way to resolve conflicts productively. Conflict resolution is the biggest obstacle to keeping people on the path toward achieving purpose. Leaders must have in place an effective means of ensuring that conflict is promptly and wisely resolved. Otherwise, leaders cannot keep people on the path. Unresolved conflict will ultimately cause strife and division that will adversely affect unity and commitment to mission.

Wise leaders and managers use the skills of every personal- or business-family member to assist the efforts of the entire family, and are careful to avoid having their relationships dominated by the following types of personalities: attention hog, dominator, blocker, diversionist, avoider. A healthy personal or business family has people responsible for action (initiators, facilitators, organizers, information collectors and evaluators) and people who play a support role (reconcilers/negotiators, protectors, encouragers and servers).

WAR AND PEACE: NEGOTIATING CONFLICTS

WISDOM MAKES US sensitive to brewing storms and gives us the inner leadership ingredients to turn clouds into sunshine.

Wisdom instructs us that a house divided against itself cannot stand. A solid personal or business family must have unity to function properly. Saint Paul's teaching can be applied to business. In this context, he taught that for harmony (unity) to be maintained, business-family members must speak the same speech. He taught that there must be no divisions among them. He taught that business-family members must be perfectly joined in the same mind and in the same judgment. Agreement means accord, harmony and resolved conflict. This, of course, applies to more traditional families as well.

Conflict is usually resolved through negotiation. The Wisdom-based negotiation process applies to the resolution of conflict among all people in personal and business relationships.

There are two stages and six golden rules in the Wisdom-based negotiation process:

STAGE 1
ESTABLISH A MUTUAL INTEREST IN RESOLVING THE CONFLICT

Golden rule 1: To resolve conflict, you must first persuade the other party that they need to negotiate.

You do this by communicating your concern for the other person. Wisdom is clear that where envy and self-seeking exist, confusion exists. Clearly, resolution starts with Wisdom from above that is pure, peaceable, gentle, willing to yield, full of mercy and without partiality or hypocrisy. Wisdom is also clear that peace comes as a result of someone first seeking to sow peace. Your motive in approaching others is simple: to resolve the conflict in a way that is wise, and thus beneficial to both parties. So the first stage and golden rule number one say you must achieve agreement from the other party that resolution of the conflict is in both of your best interests.

STAGE 2
NEGOTIATE WITH THE OTHER PARTY WITH THE PURPOSE OF RESOLVING THE CONFLICT

This is where Wisdom's five other golden rules of conflict resolution come into play—rules two through six.

Golden rule 2: Identify the problem.

You must identify the reason for conflict and the nature of the problem. The parties should agree on the crux of the problem. All parties should remember to be quick to hear, slow to speak and slow to anger.

Golden rule 3: Identify behavior of each party that contributed to the conflict.

Recent studies have shown that more than 75 percent of conflicts are based on behavioral issues rather than substantive issue. This means that how you do something is just as (maybe more) important as what you do. Agree on what behaviors or actions led to the conflict you hope to resolve.

Golden rule 4: If there is a conflict of interest, then deal with the legitimate points of conflict.

You begin by identifying those points from your perspective that are not negotiable, including, first, the principles and values of Wisdom and, second, the core beliefs, principles and values of your business or family. You then must establish from your perspective that everything else is negotiable.

Golden rule 5: Begin the negotiation with a smile.

Share your proposed solution and be willing to concede first. Build bridges with healing and forgiveness.

Golden rule 6: Enter a wise settlement that has a standard of accountability and no ambiguities, and put it in writing.

If you have conceded points, then you may have changed tasks, processes, systems, goals or objectives. Make sure they are documented and that how they apply to others is communicated to the appropriate people.

If you complete these steps, you should be able to resolve the vast majority of conflicts and will in turn create the unity and commitment necessary to achieve your purpose, vision and mission.

Sometimes you will experience situations where others refuse to negotiate. When this happens, follow Wisdom's approach. In this context, I suggest that Saint Paul teaches that when resolution cannot be achieved, you must end the relationship. If you have followed the above steps with a wise heart and servant attitude, but the other party still does not want to negotiate, then end the relationship. Do it amicably, fulfilling all obligations you have to the other party, but end it.

NUGGET OF INSPIRATION

Always do right. This will gratify some people and astonish the rest.

—Mark Twain

CHAPTER NINETEEN

TRUST IS THE CORNERSTONE OF LEADERSHIP

Whoever is careless with the truth in small matters cannot be trusted with important matters.

—Albert Einstein

Trust is the cornerstone of leadership. Without trust, leaders cannot guide others toward excellence and success. People trust leaders who communicate wisely and lead by personal example. They observe the paths leaders follow themselves. If the leaders' communication and examples demonstrate confidence, followers also gain increased confidence. Leaders are constantly influencing other people to trust or distrust them.

INFLUENCE AND LEADERSHIP COMMUNICATION

COMMITMENT MEANS dedicating yourself 100 percent, with nothing held in reserve. Commitment is good, provided it is based on Truth, the highest reality. Many of us commit our lives to pursuits that, in the final analysis, have no eternal worth. When we enter a personal, spiritual relationship commitment with God, we are shaped by highest truth—Eternal Truth. Our purpose then will yield lasting benefits in our lives and the lives of everyone we influence.

Clear and consistent communication by leaders builds unity and commitment to mission. It builds trust because it demonstrates leaders' genuine interest in others. To achieve effective, understandable communication with groups or individuals, leaders need to follow Wisdom guidelines. Wisdom will help leaders develop the required listening, hearing, speaking and writing skills to communicate effectively.

Along the path of success, leadership influence is greatly affected by how well leaders meet the four prerequisites to Wisdom-based communication:

1. What leaders communicate must always agree with the business's core beliefs, principles and values, and its purpose, vision, and mission. Make sure you use the same words consistently, in oral or written communications, and that you explain those words thoroughly when you first use them.

2. Messages are transmitted using verbal and nonverbal symbols. Make sure your nonverbal communication (e.g., body language and tone of voice) is consistent with your verbal communication. Repeat key items to make sure your audience understands them and why they are important.

3. Listen to your audience's response so that you can respond in turn and keep the lines of communication open. Your audience may be hearing your message for the first time. Take the time to field questions and explain graciously, so everyone understands your actions and why you are taking them. Then listen carefully to any more questions. It's always good to restate questions carefully so that you and the questioners can agree on what they are asking.

4. Understand the attitudes, backgrounds and beliefs of your audience, and be sure you take them into account when preparing your message. A recent study concluded that 95 percent of communication failure is caused by messages that were misunderstood because the listener's attitude, background or beliefs were not effectively addressed. Let your au-

dience know you understand their point of view and that you have taken it into account.

Maintaining leadership influence requires the employment of specific communication skills that we must strive to develop and to employ consistently with our business families. These skills will establish credibility and lead to willing cooperation from others:

1. Establish trust by demonstrating character and integrity that adhere to Wisdom's core beliefs, principles and values, as well as the purpose, vision and mission of your business.

2. Exhibit sincere compassion for other people in everything you communicate or do. Nurture your sincere desire to satisfy their interests, based on truly caring about their welfare. You cannot fake this emotion, and I strongly advise you not to try.

3. Know your audience's cultural and positional backgrounds, and shape your message accordingly. Your words should fit your audience because your goal is to communicate with them. Do not underrate or talk down to your audience. Be careful about using the personal pronoun *he*, when you are referring to both men and women. Speak to people about the things that affect them and interest them.

4. Possess a thorough knowledge of your subject matter. Understand your subject before you try to communicate about it. Explain your logic thoroughly. Be prepared for detailed questions. If you do not know an answer, tell the questioner you will find out. Then keep your word.

5. Communicate frequently and regularly in a manner that is clear, concise and specific. Use the first person singular, showing that you take responsibility for what you say. People not only want to be told about plans and planned actions, but they also want to know how plans and actions are progressing in actual application. All members of the business family want to see the big picture, not just what's in their particular areas. Schedule meetings regularly to communicate results and any circumstances that have changed since the last com-

munication. Regularly scheduled employee updates can greatly and positively influence employee behavior. The greater the changes, the more informative and frequent should be the updates.

6. Listen carefully, respond carefully and maintain an even temper by keeping excessive emotions out of the communication. Listen carefully to the questions, ponder before you respond and never, ever respond in a way that is emotionally out of control. Also control the emotions expressed in your verbal and written communication so that others will be less likely to become emotionally out of control.

7. Start meetings or written communication by reminding yourself that you will answer all questions under two conditions: that communication is mutually respectful and that discussion about persons remains limited those present.

Wisdom instructs all to be swift to hear, slow to speak and slow to wrath. It also teaches that pleasant words are sweetness to the soul and health to the bones.

LEAD BY EXAMPLE

EFFECTIVE COMMUNICATION is only the first step toward leadership influence. Effective communication must be linked directly to providing effective examples. "Do as I say, not as I do," is *not* an effective leadership strategy! In their own personal conduct in business and in the manner of personal lifestyle, effective business leaders must demonstrate what they expect of others within the organizational environment.

Guidance of others by example is the most important of all leadership functions. Leaders of bad character may pretend to be trustworthy, but their true character will eventually overcome their fabricated style, and other people's trust in them will erode. Trust is earned, and leaders must continually earn the trust of followers by acting in a manner that matches their creed.

The most influential and effective paradigm of conduct within a leader's sphere of influence is the manner of his or her personal conduct. Try these proven Wisdom-based leadership examples:

- Ask nicely.
- Compliment people who do good work. Always let employees, customers and suppliers know you appreciate them. Use every opportunity that presents itself to give deserved credit, honor and praise to others, publicly and privately.
- If employees or suppliers make mistakes or fail, correct them pleasantly and move on. Do not expect anyone to be perfect until you are!

VALUES REALLY MATTER

HERE ARE SOME examples of how non-Wisdom-based beliefs, values and principles can cause leaders to lose their influence and destroy the unity of a business family. Leaders may

- treat employees like slaves, possessions or children;
- openly violate their policies against fraternization or discrimination, but still expect their employees to demonstrate fidelity, faithfulness and loyalty to the company.

These are just a few examples of the ways in which leaders may explicitly or implicitly communicate their unwise belief that personal and business values don't mix. Some carry that a step further by saying that compassion, generosity and openly caring about others is taboo in business. I do not want to dwell on these examples because this book is about Wisdom, not folly. Yet these leadership errors are routine in many businesses.

It is important to keep in mind where these actions lead. Employees may begin to harbor unwise thoughts, such as, "The customer is only the means to our ends." Soon the customer or employee realizes this and a divergence of interests occurs. This affects business results, and soon leaders wonder why their "excellent" plan went South! A leader's unwise example may eventually cause employees not to believe anything he or she says. This leads to distrust, and distrust damages or destroys an employee's focus, diligence, and perseverance. People cannot focus effectively on a lie. We cannot be diligent in carrying out a lie. We cannot persevere in something that may change tomorrow, but is based only on the leader's whim or self-interest. Lack of focus, diligence and perseverance will result in unfulfilled business plans as well as more serious problems, such as high staff turnover, loss of valuable customers, alienated suppliers and diminished market share.

That is why trust is the cornerstone of leadership influence. If the people you are trying to influence do not trust you, they will not follow you!

NUGGETS OF INSPIRATION

Honor begets honor; trust begets trust; faith begets faith; and hope is the mainspring of life.
—Henry Lewis Stimson

Leadership is a potent combination of strategy and character. But if you must be without one, be without the strategy.
—Norman Schwarzkopf

CHAPTER TWENTY

ROCK THE BOAT

Leadership, like everything else in life that is vital, finds its source in understanding. To be worthy of management responsibility today, a man must have insight into the human heart, for unless he has an awareness of human problems, a sensitivity towards the hopes and aspirations of those whom he supervises, and a capacity for analysis of the emotional forces that motivate their conduct, the projects entrusted to him will not get ahead no matter how often wages are raised.

—Clarence Randall

Failing organizations are usually over-managed and under-led.

—Warren Bennis

LEADERSHIP IS HEART-DRIVEN

LEADERS EXERCISE a great deal of power—in business, in the community and within the family—so Wisdom-based character and integrity inside individual leaders is tantamount to lasting success in all areas of life. The personal character and integrity of individual leaders may not totally prevent compromise of beliefs, principles and values in a business, but they are moves in the direction of returning business to its rightful place of honor in our society. Leaders have the perfect platform from which to influence everyone with whom they come in contact—from colleagues to employees, subcontractors, suppliers, customers and their families. That platform is called *positional power.* The influence of leaders' beliefs, principles and values and their own personal examples are very significant. In their business conduct and manner of personal lifestyle, leaders demonstrate what they expect of others in the organization. What leaders *do* has influence, not what they *say.*

What leaders are on the inside determines what they do. The most skillfully written or inspiring oratory of leadership's vision has far, far less influence on followers than the leadership's example. Mission statements, filled with noble ideals or qualitative slogans, pale in comparison to the personal example of a business's leaders.

LEADERSHIP IS ACTION

LEADERSHIP IS THE ACT of leading and involves all these actions:

1. Guiding someone by going in advance;
2. Directing someone on a course;
3. Serving as a channel;
4. Positioning oneself at the vanguard.

The leadership role should be people oriented, not object oriented. In each business activity, leadership acts first, and the performance of the leadership role influences the performance of the succeeding roles. In this sense, leadership is guiding and directing people, through example, on a course of action.

There are three types of leaders—cautionaries, undertakers and visionaries.

I made up the term *cautionaries* to describe people who put up too many caution signs. They say things like, "Ohhhhhhhh. I am not sure we are ready for this. We have never done this before. Ohhhhhhhhh!!!!!"

Undertakers bury new ideas. They don't just put up caution signs—they put up stop signs! They say that certain new ideas and methods will never work. They are reputation conscious and financially too conservative, asking, "What if this newfangled such-and-such fails? What about the market's opinion of our company? How much is that going to knock off our equity position?" Cautionaries and undertakers are bogged down in the status quo and less than fun to be around!

I believe the best visionary leaders are those with Wisdom inside. They allow the Spirit of God to work inside them to give them the highest mental, emotional and spiritual understanding of the nature of all things. They focus on challenge and opportunity for fulfilling truly important and enduring business and life purposes. They always think about the effect of decisions on people and relationships. They ask whether the idea or change under consideration is the right thing to do for everyone concerned.

These visionary leaders believe in Saint Paul's battle cry, to press on for the highest prize of the high calling of God. Thus they have a passion for what can be, and establish the most noble goals. They ask for the highest standards for measuring the quality—not just the quantity—of individual and business performance. They are aware that their personal and business agendas are superseded by God's agenda.

THE LEADERSHIP ROLE

THE ROLE OF LEADERSHIP is to lead people and serve those who perform the management function. Leaders lead people by establishing and communicating core ideology—through personal example, vision-casting, defining and communicating the vision and mission, mentoring and training. It is every leader's Wisdom-based duty to mentor someone to take over the helm. In a family, parents mentor their children to become responsible adults, able to lead their own families in turn. Older children mentor their younger siblings to take over household tasks or to learn games and sports or to master their schoolwork. In a business, a leader can only move up when someone else is equipped to take that leader's current position. The MindSet of Wisdom gives us the confidence to mentor others to replace ourselves.

THE MANAGEMENT ROLE

THE MANAGEMENT ROLE is different from the leadership role. Management devises a strategy of how to get from point A to point B and develops a detailed plan for the trip, including specifics of the beginning point, the destination and a clearly marked road map of the best way to get there. Management also involves supervising the actions taken by those who carry out the plan. My definition of the function of the management role is very unorthodox, as you might expect, since it is based on Wisdom inside the manager.

Management's role is to fulfill the needs of those in the manager's span of control and sphere of influence. In other words, the manager serves those in the employee role and people outside the organization sphere, so they can accomplish their jobs on behalf of the business.

Management has traditionally been defined as overseeing the accomplishment of the tasks required to achieve the purpose, vision and mission of the business as defined and established by leadership.

In a business with Wisdom as its philosophical foundation, the management role is much broader than just overseeing people and tasks. Wisdom-based management requires the ability to discern inner qualities and relationships, act with good sense and pursue a wise course of action. A truly wise manager will continually test the means he or she develops to ensure that they are in perfect alignment with Wisdom's core beliefs, principles, values and priorities.

THE LEADERSHIP HEARTSKILL
AND MINDSET OF WISDOM

THE HEARTSKILL AND MINDSET of Wisdom enhance leadership in our personal and on-the-job relationships and responsibilities. The pathway to excellence and to lasting success in our personal and business lives is paved with the flagstones of Wisdom, Honor and Hope, the three precious inner stones and blessings of a spiritually wise heart. Such a heart possesses the HeartSkill of Wisdom, which creates the MindSet of Wisdom.

Wisdom's selfless gracious-servant principle is an essential component of leadership. According to this principle, leaders should serve others, on and off the job. Many leaders try to operate by different philosophies. They have yet to learn that spiritual values at home and work definitely do mix—one way or the other. Leadership's beliefs, principles and values end up impacting others, inside and outside the professional sphere.

ONE'S POSITION IN A BUSINESS IS MUCH LESS IMPORTANT THAN ONE'S *DIS*POSITION

ACCORDING TO MATTHEW, leaders become tyrants when they arrogantly use authority and power to manipulate, suppress, control and use subordinates for the leader's self-serving advantage only. But we can avoid being tyrants controlled by the self-serving mindset by seeking guidance in Wisdom, where we will find the selfless gracious-servant principle described by Jesus when he said that anyone who wants to be a leader must first be a servant to those he or she seeks to lead. Wise leaders figure out how to best serve subordinates and all within their span of control and sphere of influence. Leaders should always use their position, authority and power according to the selfless gracious-servant principle to provide lasting benefits to others.

Wisdom-based leadership, then, is guiding and directing the business and the people who make up the business, on a wise course of action. This can be done *only* from a spiritually wise heart that commands a servant attitude of mind, and will lead to both outstanding business profits and enduring benefits for all affected by wise leadership. What others see and perceive you as being is what counts, not what you say or what you know. Leaders who get real satisfaction and ultimate fulfillment are the ones who reach out beyond themselves to demonstrate real love, care and concern for everyone they influence.

If you should doubt this, I urge you to answer the following question. When someone loves you unconditionally and treats you with respect and dignity, what is your sense of respect, duty and loyalty to that person?

LEADERSHIP STYLES

WISDOM INSTRUCTS us regarding four leadership styles, to be used in four distinct types of circumstances:

1
DICTATORIAL STYLE

Use for organizational or personal crisis and major disciplinary matters.

2
AUTHORITATIVE STYLE

Use in a one-person operation, with new hires, and for situations involving business policy, rules and regulations.

3
CONSULTATIVE STYLE

Use for planning or problem-solving requiring creativity or innovation, and for routine matters in day-to-day operations.

4
PARTICIPATIVE STYLE

Use this style to motivate highly competent, proven employees in preparation and planning activities and situations requiring creativity and innovation.

Wise leaders give and share to help others reach their dreams. They know that the eternal rewards of following Wisdom are more important than receiving accolades, financial remuneration and all the other foolish rewards chased by people who are still choosing the self-serving mindset. Being the best leader possible is an ever-continuing journey to attend to the needs of others. And it's a journey of great joy and happiness.

People who are served and led by leaders who practice Wisdom are affected in a very powerful and positive way. They voluntarily and enthusiastically act to serve those whose leadership is Wisdom-based. People respect leaders who demonstrate unconditional love and respect for others.

The dictatorial style of leadership, and often the authoritative style, breed every conceivable bad attitude in subordinates when used in all situations. These styles appeal to negative emotions and feelings. Little wonder that they cause constant problems in business, in families and in other kinds of organizations. Most people will do as little as possible for title-slinging, card-toting and list-flashing drill-sergeant types, but they will cut cartwheels and leap over tall buildings in a single bound for the provider and protector-leader.

G. L. Banks wrote in *The Aim,* "I live for those who love me, for those who know me true; / For the heaven that smiles above me, and awaits my spirit, too. / For the cause that lacks assistance, for the wrong that needs resistance; / For the future in the distance, and the good I can do."

That's Wisdom-based leadership.

FAMILY CULTURE

WHEN HELEN KELLER said that the welfare of each is bound up in the welfare of all, she could have been talking about what I call Family Culture. The principles of Wisdom make leaders responsible for creating an environment of shared purpose, vision and mission. The Family Culture is a unified choir of many voices producing highest success, where every family member's talents are fully appreciated and used.

Wisdom is clear that leadership should promote a business culture based on Family Culture, not simply a team concept. I call this the business–Family Culture. The common elements that can establish the Family Culture in a business are the HeartSkill and MindSet of Wisdom. Team emphasis, rather than business-family focus, tends to promote division. A business–Family Culture promotes the unity needed for highest and most enduring success. The practical day-to-day keys to developing and maintaining a Family Culture in any business of any size and kind are these:

1. Leaders must view themselves, employees, customers and suppliers as a family; and
2. The business itself, and each leader, manager and employee, must possess and apply the HeartSkill and MindSet of Wisdom in all business matters. Remember, the MindSet of Wisdom is characterized by specific inner qualities: Wisdom, Honor and Hope.

With Wisdom inside the business-family members, the common features include the same role and relationship philosophy (Wisdom's enduring precepts and principles). Each family member possesses and is guided by common motive (unconditional love), common passion (serving others' best interests first), and common values (inner character and integrity). These common cultural features show up in each business-family member's personality as an inner and outer graciousness that I call Wisdom's amazing disposition. The value of the gracious goodness of Wisdom's amazing disposition applies to business roles and relationships as much as it applies to personal roles and relationships.

Unconditional love is the power that overcomes dissension and strife. This love binds people together in unity and creates synergy, which is far, far superior to other powers and motives in business operations. The unity of people within an organization depends on the strength of its underlying power.

BUSINESS–FAMILY CULTURE

WISDOM INSTRUCTS that if one family member is honored, all the other family members celebrate the honor. Highest success is achieved when individuals are concerned with the family and not focused on who gets the credit. Wisdom carries the business–Family Culture concept even further. It includes within the family circle of the business all those with whom the business and employees create interactions, including customers, prospects and suppliers.

If one part of the business family is experiencing something, then all the other family members will eventually experience it, too. For instance, imagine that Slim Pickpocket, over in the shipping department, is scarfing every third unit and selling it on the side, pocketing the money for himself. Can we agree that other members of Slim's business family would experience the impact of that?

Or what if Mary, in the secretarial pool, has the flu and her peers (all the other business-family members) do not help out while she is absent? Can we agree that her business family, and Mary, too, will eventually experience the consequences? Who counts more in the overall success of the company? Is it Mary or Slim or the company's leadership?

Let me answer that question with another story from my life.

When I was twenty-three years old and full of myself and the philosophies of folly, I was appointed chief financial officer for a publicly held company that traded on NASDAQ. My first day on the job, I thought it would be good to lay down "the law according to Cecil." So I called all the accounting, data processing and financial staff in, and I put on an Oscar-caliber, dictatorial-style performance. I concluded by stating that anyone in the room who could not live by "Mr. Most Important's" rules and regulations should just go ahead and leave. When I stopped talking, the silence in the room was almost palpable. No one moved or said a word. I took that as my cue to approach the stage to accept my well-deserved Oscar.

As I basked in the glow of my power, Freddie, our only keypunch operator, said, "I will be leaving now."

Translation: She quit. *That* announcement sobered me up pretty quickly! Whom do you suppose that room full of employees thought was the more important family member, Freddie or me? Whom do you suppose I thought was most important at that moment? Freddie, of course.

Talk about learning a public lesson about how leaders and employees belong to one family of equally important members! Freddie put everything in perspective. I consumed several large humble pies in the process of persuading Freddie to stay.

The sad part was that, back then, I was only pretending to be humble and pretending to have learned the lesson. True Wisdom applied in the business world was still a foreign concept to me.

Wisdom asks a simple question: "Are you a member of the family?" If you are, then all family members are your peers, and you and they all count equally toward the overall success of the organization. Wisdom inside will cause all leaders and all employees to stop defining the value of each family member's contribution based on false measures such as salary or title.

UNITY

UNLESS LEADERS CAN create and maintain unity, all their other leadership and management skills are essentially worthless to the organization. Unity manifests as good relationships; a pleasant, friendly, productive and efficient work environment; a true Family Culture and spirit among leaders, managers, other employees, customers and suppliers. The beginning point of business unity is leadership and management from a spiritually wise heart that creates and commands a servant attitude. A spiritually wise heart and servant attitude causes leaders and managers to focus first on what should be first—meeting the needs of others. Employee spirit, company morale and other individual and group dynamics are clear indications of whether unity exists or not in a business.

Wisdom is very clear that a house divided against itself cannot stand. It tells us that we cannot serve two masters. That instruction can be applied in many ways.

Real power is power united. Strength is in unity, while grave danger lurks in disharmony. Business systems and processes, while important, mean little if the people who use them follow folly's beliefs and principles in their conduct. The integrity of systems depends on the integrity of the people working within those systems. Beliefs, principles and values are more important than planning or business systems. If you want something done well, be sure the person doing it believes and habitually follows Wisdom. Who does the task is far less relevant than the person's beliefs and values.

PEOPLE AND RELATIONSHIPS COME FIRST

WISE LEADERS FOCUS on people and relationships, not only on goals. The only reason we formulate and seek to maintain relationships is because we have unmet needs that we perceive can be met through forming relationships. By "needs," I mean the specific desires and requirements of parties on both ends of the relationship. When needs are met in relationships, then those relationships flourish. When needs are not met, relationships suffer and often break. Relationships in which needs are met on a one-sided basis are doomed to eventual failure.

Relationships may be characterized as cooperative, aggressive, manipulative or alienating. Almost all philosophies for personal, relationship, and leadership guidance teach us to compete with each other, as the supreme expression of inner passion. Wisdom's perfectly excellent action is cooperation for the good of all. We all share the goal of getting things done. How we go about getting things done is crucially important. When we put ourselves before others, we create situations in which something may get done, but people may get hurt and relationships may be damaged. This is unwise. Cooperation does not operate that way. Cooperation gets the job done, while edifying and encouraging others. Being cooperative builds and preserves consensus and vital personal and business relationships. Wisdom rejects aggressive, manipulative and alienating approaches and behavior. Instead, Wisdom instructs us to value people's total well-being and unbroken, harmonious relationships.

To do that in the real business world requires a cooperative, family environment, in which leaders not only recognize that theory, but also establish it and maintain it in practice. Wise leaders value a cooperative environment, offering praise, recognition and acknowledgment. These Wisdom principles nurture creativity and imagination and allow business-family members to feel they can fail without suffering the adverse consequences that abound in competition-driven business environments. When leaders use fear to motivate employees, they stifle productivity, efficiency and innovation. Wisdom in leadership nurtures growth, creativity and learning; it views failure as an opportunity to learn and grow.

Leaders who create an environment that gives people the opportunity to demonstrate their talents are often amazed at their employees' latent gifts—gifts that can make a phenomenal difference to business productivity and efficiency. This produces long-term positive results when leaders subscribe to the business-family model.

CREATIVITY AND INNOVATION

WHEN THE PHILOSOPHY of Wisdom and its principles and values form the foundation of your business, you have the best platform possible for "Eureka!" and "What if . . ." to occur regularly. Wisdom can change the course of the company—for the better. The greatest gains in individual and business productivity and efficiency come from creative ideas. Creativity and innovation have zero overhead. Using them wisely costs nothing, but not using them can cost a bundle. *The wise leader promotes a Family Culture in which people are encouraged to grow and expand and where they are given psychological ownership of the organization.* They bring out creativity and foster innovation. Wise leaders know that God has blessed everyone in the family with huge innovative and creative capabilities. Leaders or managers can promote a business-family environment in which creativity and innovation flourish because people feel needed. When their desire to be wanted is satisfied and problems are solved, business efficiency improves and productivity soars.

WE'RE ALL IN THE SERVICE SECTOR

WISDOM INSTRUCTS that the leader's role is to serve subordinates, customers and suppliers. Leadership does not exist to be served. Every member of the business family should live to serve the others. This should be each family member's passion. Wisdom instructs each of us that we are all equal in importance to achieving the end purpose and that our passion should be making others lives more pleasant, tolerable and productive. Be there for others, but give them freedom to be different from you. Have relationships that are strong enough to weather the clouds and storms that come your way. Don't be ashamed to openly show your positive and sensitive feelings of care and concern for those in your business family.

Unconditional love means sharing responsibilities and credit equally, as a family. Work together toward common goals. Help each other along the Inner Path to True Greatness. Treat every day at work as a special day. Do not take other business-family members for granted. Take time to talk; take time to plant some roses, and come back often to water them. Don't take out your frustrations on another person. Above all, follow Wisdom's principles, embrace its values and be open to the spiritually uplifting Wisdom Truth that is all around you.

Little things become big, one way or another, whether constructively or destructively. Good family relationships—business or personal—require time, sharing and devotion. Wisdom-based relationships—business or personal—require that we sacrifice ourselves and our way for others. When we band together for common purpose, our business and each member of the family can achieve truly lasting success. The dynamic power and synergy of a united entity is an amazing thing. And an entity united with God's purpose can truly serve and change the world—one person at a time.

NUGGET OF INSPIRATION

The person who will be the leader must be servant of all.
—(personal paraphrase of) Jesus

AFTERWORD

A BEAUTIFUL JOURNEY OF CHANGE

I'm going to a special place when I die. But I want to be sure my life is special while I'm here.

—Payne Stewart

Life can be a beautiful journey when we open our hearts to Wisdom and the influence of the Spirit of God. Then a wise heart can reprogram our character and thinking. We don't always like change, but we must learn to welcome change if we want to see improvement in our lives. Most of us understand perfectly what Albert Einstein meant when he said that problems cannot be solved by the same level of thinking that created them, but we are so content with or complacent in our current ways of thinking, we refuse to make the effort to rise to the next level of thinking. If we keep doing things the same old way according to high-sounding but completely powerless and empty philosophies of folly, we will keep on getting the same results.

We can change our choices. We must not set our aspirations, goals and priorities by what others value and find desirable. *Being* great inside must precede *doing* great. Wisdom teaches us that making a life is far more valuable than making a living and having lots of money and possessions. Changing who we are and how we see on the inside will change how we act, how we react, how we think—literally *how we live.*

When you live with God inside, you can't help but influence other people. That influence may not be apparent for a long time. That's okay. Your job is not to monitor—just to live right, love right and trust in the Divine's ways. This is so hard if you are a parent. Sometimes, no matter what we do, our children go off the beaten path and choose roads that we feel are not in their best interest. Once we have done all we can do as parents, we need to stand still, believing with faith that God will see them through safely. A parent's *nature* is to want to protect and make better any situation we see as harmful for our children. A parent's *job* is to teach Wisdom to our children and to welcome the change in our relationship as they become independent travelers on the Inner Path to True Greatness.

You give the precious stone . . . you pray . . . and you wait . . .

ON A PERSONAL NOTE

MOM AND DAD—this book is, in large part, a thank-you to you. Thank you for giving me the best love, precious stone of God's Way and Wisdom so long ago . . . and thank you for patiently waiting for me to see the Light and learn those lessons.

I'm an ol' country boy at heart. From the country song, "Lessons Learned" (performed by Tracy Lawrence and written by him and by Paul Nelson and Larry Boone), here is my tribute to one who walked the Inner Path to True Greatness—my dad—Big C (Granddaddy to his many grand- and great-grandchildren). Big C, if I had five minutes with you on this side of eternity, I'd sing it personally—and I know you wouldn't say a thing about my horrible singing voice!

> *Granddaddy was a man I loved*
> *He bought me my first ball and glove*
> *He even taught me how to drive his truck*
> *Circling around that old town square*
> *He spoke of life in a slow southern drawl*
> *But I never heard him cause I thought I knew it all*

You can bet I listened though
When the call came that he was no longer there

Lessons learned sure run deep
They don't go away and they don't come cheap
There's no way around it
This world turns on lessons learned

Cecil Sr., I will always love you and be grateful, from the bottom of my heart, for the privilege and honor of being your son. One of these days I'm comin' home to see you! We're all coming home! As the old hymn reminds us, What a reunion that's gonna be. Meet me in the morning, on the shores of your new and eternal home, in Beulah, the land they call forever.

FOLLOW YOUR DREAM

FOUR YEARS AGO, in my introspection after my father's death, I felt God impressing me to share with others on a full-time basis the Philosophy of Wisdom I had developed and practiced in my personal and business life for almost two decades. Talk about resisting change! Now I can joke and laugh about it, but back then I got an A+ in digging my heels in and resisting to the max!

"See the good in change?" I protested. "See that things are changing for the better? Are you crazy, God? No way! Look, I am a successful businessman," I said to God. "I don't want to leave that world, one where I know the likely result of every step I take. I'll write some and share more, but full-time? You're kidding, right, God?"

No, God was not kidding! I stopped talking and began to listen to the prompting of the Divine within. Eventually I took my own advice. I saw the Hope in change.

When we accept the good in change, when we see change as a hopeful part of our existence, we embrace change as opportunity to grow and become better. As I wrote this version of the manuscript of *Wisdom Honor & Hope,* Patty and I completed the sale of what had been our principal business during the past decade and a half. So you can call me "Mr. Full-time." Sold out, and loving every minute of it! I do not know that I have gotten better as a writer, but I know I have grown as a person. Talk about inverted learning curves! I am like the pilot flying upside down in an old crop duster. I may be killing the King's English, and the odd reader, too, but I am having the time of my life, because I am living my passion and because I feel that, again I am fulfilling God's purpose for my life.

THANK YOU, PATIENT READER

THANK YOU for buying and reading this book.

My prayer for you is for the God of Hope to fill you with Divine hope, peace and joy that will overflow into every life you influence and touch, for that is the gift of true greatness. When you leave on the light of the Divine, it will shine from within, and you will make the most positive impressions on others and give them an enduring legacy of great value. When you release yourself to the true reality of your purpose and mission, Wisdom, Honor and Hope will fill your being, direct your work and bless others. You will walk the Inner Path to True Greatness. You will live with significance and meaning. You will shine with God's love.

Please believe and follow your path. The rest of us need you. And remember, when our lives are committed to fulfillment of eternal purpose, we achieve our waking dreams and sleeping hopes. Nothing compares to the promise of your life in partnership with God.

NUGGET OF INSPIRATION

When I stand before God at the end of my life, I would hope that I would not have a single bit of talent left and could say, "I used everything you gave me."

—Erma Bombeck

APPENDIX
OF

WISDOM TRUTH

Wisdom is found only in truth.
—Johann Wolfgang von Goethe

Truth is not a crystal that you can stash away in your pocket, it is an infinite liquid into which you fall.
—Robert von Musil

This Appendix shares more of my discoveries of Wisdom Truth. As in chapter two, they are listed under the five core beliefs of the Philosophy of Wisdom. Do remember that (1) my working definition of Wisdom Truth is something spoken, expressed or discovered by Spirit-led people down through history that is consistent with the Eternal Truth of the Bible; and (2) I have paraphrased biblical stories, authors and texts in an attempt to make this book more readily understood in today's language. The quotations in the Appendix are all paraphrases.

THE PHILOSOPHY OF WISDOM'S CORE BELIEFS

1
THE POWER SOURCE FOR A LIFE BUILT ON THE PHILOSOPHY OF WISDOM IS GOD

Trying to attain personal spirituality through observation of a set of rules can be very frustrating, and is never successful. Just when we think we've done it, along comes someone who rains on our parade by sharing how we misunderstood the rules or missed one. Personal spirituality is the result of connection to God, one-to-one through personal faith in that One True God. It is not about man-made doctrine or about rules or about what we can become or do without that connection to God.

I see the stars, I hear the rolling thunder,
Thy power throughout the universe displayed.
Then sings my soul, my savior God, to thee,
How great thou art!

—Stuart Hine

The life of significance is the one that thirsts after God. Its passion is to know Him intimately.

To drink is a small matter. To be thirsty is everything.

—Georges Duamel

Knowing God results in every other kind of understanding.

To know that what is impenetrable to us really exists,
manifesting itself as the highest wisdom and the most
radiant beauty . . .

—Albert Einstein

Where you choose to place your attention has a great influence on the direction of your life.

Perfect peace is the reward of the person whose mind is
focused, totally concentrated on God.

—Isaiah

Patience acknowledges that God is in control and that things are just as they need to be, right now, this moment, even if we are not able to see the purpose in all that is going on around us.

There are times when God asks nothing of His children except silence, patience and tears.
—Charles Seymour Robinson

Faith in God creates in us real Hope—inner certainty, security and assurance—which overcomes all fear of death and inspires us to live in union with Him.

For you alone, Lord God, are worthy of our worship.
—John

A relationship with the Divine provides loving arms that can help you through any situation, giving you complete access to His vast reservoir of strength, comfort and peace.

The eternal God is your refuge, and God's everlasting arms, your foundational support.
—Moses

Highest Faith is being certain of the Divine. That confidence is the basis of a higher viewpoint of life where only the very best is expected, now and into eternity.

Nothing splendid has ever been achieved except by those who dared believe that something inside them was superior to circumstance.
—Bruce Barton

Highest Wisdom, Honor and Hope are held in the heart of those who trust and reverence God and allow those "being" gifts from the Divine Spirit within to guide all decisions. In other words, they become a higher being.

The need for devotion to something outside ourselves is even more profound than the need for companionship.
—Ross Parmenter

God's presence is everywhere—in the home, on the street, in the market, in the workplace—anywhere people, science and nature are found.

This is well-nigh the greatest of discoveries a man can make, that God is not confined in churches, but that the streets are sacred because His presence is there, that the market-place is one of His abiding places, and ought, therefore, to be a sanctuary. Any moment in any place, the veil can suddenly grow thin and God be seen.

—R. C. Gillie

God fills our lives with good things. Life's blessings prove God's, not our, greatness.

I asked God for all things that I may enjoy life; God gave me life that I may enjoy all things.

—unknown

2
TRUE WISDOM, PURPOSE AND JOY COME FROM LOVING GOD, LISTENING TO GOD, LOVING YOURSELF AND SERVING OTHERS

Thou shalt love the Lord thy God with all thy heart, and with all thy soul, and with all thy mind. This is the first and great commandment. And the second is like unto it, Thou shalt love thy neighbor as thyself.

—Jesus

Honor who you are as a creation of God, as part of the master plan, one very important piece of an infinite puzzle and a unique and very special part of the whole.

Attaining an intimate, personal relationship with the Divine will move your life upward to highest significance.

Live to please God and He will breathe on thee His peace.

—F. B. Meyer

Dedication to the Divine and His purpose is the power behind true progress—advancements in relationships and the welfare of humanity—that stands the test of time.

The high destiny of the individual is to serve rather than to rule.

—Albert Einstein

Some things you can count, don't really count. Some things you cannot count, really count.

—Albert Einstein

A life well lived is one of devotion to partnership with God, in love and service to others.

This is the true joy of life; being used for a purpose recognized in yourself as a mighty one!
—George Bernard Shaw

It is possible to love others unconditionally, only with God's love within and Divine grace to help us. When we are in harmonious personal relationship and partnership with the Divine, we are full of love and grace that gives. As we love God and know and feel Divine love and grace, we radiate them and are inspired by boundless and limitless motive to serve others. The best love is the love we give!

Where love is concerned, too much is not even enough.
—Pierre-Augustin Caron de Beaumarchais

Highest prosperity is the result of becoming exceptional at the ordinary.

Do ordinary things with extraordinary love.
—Mother Teresa

To find the path to true success and the highest heights, we must tend to tiny seedlings by mirroring and reflecting the light of the Creator's love to the smallest of His Shining Stars. These are the seedlings that greet and bless us on the path to true success.

The test of our progress is not whether we add more to the abundance of those who have much; it is whether we provide enough for those who have too little.
—Franklin Roosevelt

In our difficulties, we can learn to identify with others' pain. Then we can comfort others in their times of pain, giving them hope, pleasing our Maker and creating a legacy of Love.

I never ask the wounded person how he feels; I myself become the wounded person.
—Walt Whitman

In the likeness of God, our compassion should be interwoven into everything we say and do.

> *The widest thing in the universe is not space; it is the potential capacity of the human heart. Being made in the image of God, it is capable of almost unlimited extension in all directions.*
>
> —A. W. Tozer

Love beyond human reasoning and understanding. Unconditional love releases the need to understand the person, situation or anything else.

> *The art of being wise is the art of knowing what to overlook.*
>
> —William James

Unconditional love is the wellspring of motivation and passion to do the greater good. Love thinks before speaking. Love overlooks insults. Love forgets mistakes.

Unconditional love knows and does just one thing—it loves.

> *Don't give what is left over. Give what costs you. Give until it hurts.*
>
> —Mother Teresa

We honor others when we recognize their gifts to us.

> *The greatest good you can do for another is not just to share your riches but to reveal to him his own.*
>
> —Benjamin Disraeli

We are blessed to be a blessing to others. The freedom to love and serve each other cannot be taken from us.

> *When nothing else could help,*
> *Love lifted me.*
>
> —Howard E. Smith/ James Rowe

Life's greatest accomplishments are the result of reckless abandon to the Divine working through us.

> *Do all the good you can, in all the ways you can, in all the places you can, at all the times you can, for all the people you can.*
>
> —John Wesley

Wisdom leads us to focus our attention outward, sharing in unselfish service to others.

Whatever measure you use to give, large or small, will be used to measure what is given back to you.

—Jesus

How easy it is to forget to treat our loved ones with kindness and courtesy. We seem to reserve our best behavior for strangers and formal occasions. Love, intimacy and familiarity are not excuses for neglecting to say "please" and "thank you," and for offering those wonderful, unsolicited compliments that light up a person's day.

We've got this gift of love, but love is like a precious plant. You can't just accept it and leave it in the cupboard or just think it's going to get on by itself. You've got to keep watering it; really look after it and nurture it.

—John Lennon

The highest and best uses of money are doing good and improving souls. A legacy of love is more valuable and far more enduring than one of money and possessions.

Nothing that you have not given away will ever really be yours.

—C. S. Lewis

Kind words and praise cost nothing and accomplish much.

No act of kindness, no matter how small, is ever wasted.
—Aesop, "The Lion and the Mouse"

Going far beyond the call of duty, doing more than others expect . . . this is what excellence is all about.

We are here to add what we can to life, not to get what we can from it.

—William Osler

We belong to each other and each needs the other.

Lord, make me an instrument of Your peace!
Where there is hatred, let me sow love.
—Saint Francis of Assisi

True happiness comes to those who are just, good and fair to others.

Happiness is a by-product of an effort to make someone else happy.

—Gretta Brooker Palmer

Live so that you can hold a mirror up to yourself . . . and smile.

Wise people, even though all laws were abolished, would still lead the same life.

—Aristophanes

The ideals which have lighted me on my way, and time and time again given me new courage to face life cheerfully, have been Truth, Goodness and Beauty.

—Albert Einstein

3
WE ARE A COMBINATION OF THE PHYSICAL AND THE SPIRITUAL, AND WE MUST ACKNOWLEDGE AND EXPERIENCE *BOTH* TO LIVE FULLY

Wisdom enables us by giving us guidance and the tools for wise decision making. Wisdom ennobles us with compassion, thoughtfulness and generosity. Wisdom inspires us with the Divine presence within.

Blessed Assurance . . .
Heir of salvation, purchase of God
Born of His Spirit.

—Fanny Crosby

By choosing to conform to the ways of inner spirituality, we can become all we were created to become. True greatness is leaving the impression of the Divine on all we influence. With sorrow and pain comes a reconnection to the spirit that cries out for peace. If we find that peace, we change the world—spirit by spirit.

Hope is a state of mind, not a state of the world.

—Václav Havel

The mind is merely a reasoning device that takes heart-held beliefs, principles and values, and programs the mind with models for making choices.

To wisdom belongs understanding of eternal things;
to knowledge, the rational knowledge of temporal things.
—Saint Augustine

The most productive and enjoyable interpretation of life is not intellectual, but heartfelt.

It is only with the heart that one can see rightly, what is essential is invisible to the eye.
—Antoine de Saint-Exupéry

Our deeds should be as good as our ideals. Real love is seen in actions.

Our duty to God is to make of ourselves the most perfect product of divine incarnation that we can become. This is possible only through the pursuit of worthy ideas.
—Edgar White Burrill

Dreams birthed on mountaintops become reality walking by faith in life's valleys and on its plains.

If you have built castles in the air, your work need not be lost; that is where they should be. Now put foundations under them.
—Henry David Thoreau

Happiness is found when we don't spend all our precious time making a living, but remember to take time to breathe and really live.

There are nine requisites for contented living: Health enough to make work a pleasure; Wealth enough to support your needs; Strength enough to battle with difficulties and forsake them; Grace enough to confess your sins and overcome them; Patience enough to toil until some good is accomplished; Charity enough to see some good in your neighbor; Love enough to make you useful and helpful to

others, Faith enough to make real the things of God; Hope enough to remove all anxious fears concerning the future.
—Johann Wolfgang von Goethe

A spiritually wise heart is essential to healthy bodies, emotions, thoughts, attitudes and relationships.

Give me beauty in the inward soul; may the outward and the inward be at one.
—Socrates

4
THE LIFE-CHANGING POWER OF PRAYER IS REAL

Each act of love is both a prayer and an answer to prayer.

Modern society distracts us from life's most important activities, teaching us to fill our inner voids with things like work, entertainment and recreation. All these are necessary, but our inner spirit-person is better filled by allowing the Divine Spirit to live within the inner room of the soul. This gives God that special, private space for our prayer and continual communing with the Divine Spirit within.

Sweet hour of prayer! Sweet hour of prayer!
That calls me from a world of care,
And bids me at my Father's throne
Make all my wants and wishes known;
In seasons of distress and grief,
My soul has often found relief.
—William A. Walford

Prayer is an invisible tool that can make a very visible difference.

More things are wrought by prayer
Than this world dreams of.
—Lord Alfred Tennyson

Prayer is the best preparation for daily living and working.

Prayer should be the key of the day and the lock of the night.
—Thomas Fuller

In prayer and meditation, we connect directly to the Divine's thoughts and ways.

Faith is a gift of God and grows through prayer, as do hope and love—and those three are the main virtues of the interior life.

—Mother Teresa

Into the silence of our hearts, the Divine speaks. Don't be afraid of silence. Silence is the doorway to a peaceful state, the opportunity to block out the noise of modern life and listen to what God is saying to and through us.

God is the friend of silence. Trees, flowers, grass grow in silence.
See the stars, moon, and sun, how they move in silence.

—Mother Teresa

Prayer may be properly viewed as spiritual mealtime. In fact, prayer is fuel of the soul, a spiritual lifeline analogous to the way blood is our physical lifeline. Just as the body cannot survive without new blood, the spirit must have the fresh fuel of prayer several times a day.

God answers our prayers. Sometimes the answer is yes. Sometimes the answer is no. Sometimes the answer is, you've got to be kidding!

—Jimmy Carter

When we take the steps to establish our connection to God, the Divine Spirit literally comes to live in us, creating a brand-new person inside and beginning a new life. Divine goodness, attitudes, skill and power then reside in us. Effectively, we are clothed with a new nature of inner greatness that outwardly produces true success in our lives and all we influence.

Prayer catapults us onto the frontier of the spiritual life. Of all the spiritual disciplines prayer is the most central. . . . Real prayer is life creating and life changing.

—Richard Foster

Prayer has ripple effects in the lake of lives. Some waves are slow, gentle and easy. Others are not so. Both are good for all whose lives the prayer waves touch.

Prayer is the song of the heart. It reaches the ear of God even if it is mingled with the cry and the tumult of a thousand men.

—Kahlil Gibran

Significance is found in serving others. One of the easiest and yet most effective ways to serve others is to love them enough to pray for them daily.

Ask, and it shall be given you; seek, and ye shall find; knock, and it shall be opened unto you.

—Jesus

Those who pray together, stay together. Prayer is the bond that holds together lives, relationships, families and organizations.

Faith is an activity; it is something that has to be applied.
—Corrie Ten Boom

Prayer helps us strike a proper balance between Heaven's daily calling to a contemplative time of preparation for Earth's practical life of loving and serving others.

Prayer is a very good time for saying, "God, I'm sorry," and also for examining our hearts to determine whom we need to forgive and whom to ask forgiveness from.

And forgive us our trespasses as we forgive those who trespass against us.

—The Lord's Prayer

Close your eyes, listen to your heart . . . and remember. Speak—pray—to the Divine who has created you. Reconnect and become anew.

Expressing gratitude for all we have and experience is a powerful spiritual exercise.

One single grateful thought raised to heaven is the most perfect prayer.

—G. E. Lessing

Choose gratitude, and you will attract abundance into your life.

Those who thank God much are truly wealthy. So our inner happiness depends not on what we experience but on the degree of our gratitude to God, whatever the experience.
—Albert Schweitzer

Alone time with the Divine brings everything into proper perspective.

Being alone regularly can be a wonderful gift. It's a great opportunity to learn more about ourselves, and also to listen to God.

Anyone who imagines he can simply begin meditating without praying for the desire and the grace to do so, will soon give up.
—Thomas Merton

5
WE ARE ASSURED OF GUIDANCE AND HELP

You are never truly alone. God's Spirit is always with you.

Called or not called, God is Present.
—carved on a stone tablet over Carl Jung's door

Truth opens your eyes to new beauty and your ears to new music.

Truth releases you to a heightened reality of meaning and Hope.

Recognize and be filled with Truth when you hear it. This will bring you wisdom.

Believe on that Truth through Faith. This will bring you Hope.

Act on that Truth. This will bring you peace and joy.

Your word is a lamp unto my feet, and a light unto my path.
—David

With Divine guidance and the gifts of Wisdom, Honor and Hope, we find an inner peace and simplicity that allow us to handle our complex lives with assured faith and strong character.

Every blade of grass has its angel that bends over it and whispers, "Grow, grow."

—The Talmud

It is a wise habit to enjoy the companionship of those who love, reverence and serve God.

Disillusionment can be the gateway of the most important frontier of life: Spiritual Awakening. At that gate, we can change our direction and choose to discover our Divine potential—pursuing higher purpose and moving toward genuine fulfillment.

Unrest of spirit is a mark of life.

—Mark Menninger

The wise heart is always open to new ideas, looking for them everywhere. Listening is the first step in learning.

The real voyage of discovery consists not in seeking new landscapes, but in having new eyes.

—Marcel Proust

Think about Divine truths, store them in the heart; securely there, these are respected guides for achieving life's best dreams.

Human salvation demands the divine disclosure of truths surpassing reason.

—Saint Thomas Aquinas

Internalized, eternal Truth and the Spirit of God are light for seeing and attaining highest insight, enlightenment and understanding and likewise are wisest and most honorable and hopeful counselors.

God, grant me the serenity to accept the things I cannot change, courage to change the things I can, and the wisdom to know the difference.

—Reinhold Niebuhr

To grow, we must heal and to heal, we must let go.

To live is to be slowly born.

—Antoine de Saint-Exupéry

Our unique talents and special purpose are revealed and perfected in the middle of life's most difficult moments. In them we discover new strengths.

Believe that life is worth living, and your belief will help create the fact.

—William James

Pain often is a source of inspiration and a teacher of wisdom.

When a door of happiness closes, another door opens; but often we look so long at the door that closed, that we do not see the one that has been opened for us.

—Helen Keller

There are times in life when the why becomes irrelevant; the lesson we learn from what happens is what becomes important.

Doubt is the vestibule which all must pass before they can enter the temple of wisdom.

—Charles Colton

One cannot avoid growing older, but one does not have to become old.

For age is opportunity no less than youth itself.
—Henry Wadsworth Longfellow

We turn, not older with years, but newer every day.
—Emily Dickinson

With the inner sunshine of Eternal Truth as our Light and always in our line of vision, we never lose sight of our highest aspirations and wisely move each day toward them.

There is one spectacle grander than the sky, that is the interior of the soul.

—Victor Hugo

Eternal truths are joyous treasures and the wisdom and understanding to honorably apply them, is more valuable than silver or gold.

Searching for the truth is the noblest occupation of man; its publication is a duty.

—Madame De Staël

We are wise to learn to live daily, by the vision seen in moments of inspiration.

They are never alone that are accompanied by noble thoughts.

—Philip Sydney

Reading is to the mind what exercising is to the body.

You think your pain and heartbreak are unprecedented in the history of the world, but then you read. It was books that taught me that the things that tormented me most were the very things that connected me with all the people who were alive, or who had ever been alive.

—James Baldwin

Forgiveness is the finding again of a lost possession.

—Friedrich Schiller

Things that matter most must never be at the mercy of things that matter least.

—Johann Wolfgang von Goethe

It is not the answer that enlightens, but the question.

—Eugène Ionesco

Money can't buy me love.

—John Lennon & Paul McCartney

Be happy. It is a way of being wise.

—Colette

Eternal Truth is the only compass we need for guiding our daily living and working. It is constantly pointing up, to remind us and inspire us that our lives have higher purpose.

Be glad of life because it gives you the chance to love and to work and to play and to look up at the stars.

—Henry Van Dyke

Life is a circle. The seeds we sow become the harvest we reap.

I can feel the sufferings of millions; and yet, if I look up into the heavens, I think that it will all come right, that this cruelty will end, and that peace and tranquility will return again.

—Anne Frank

Reflect on Truth . . . and then reflect the Truth.

Begin and end every day by connecting with the Divine Spirit and renewing the soul. Embrace the nourishment of Wisdom. Breathe in the purity of Truth, inhaling its peace and hope.

Tucked deep in our heart, the Hope of Wisdom gets us through the storms and the ordinary days of life, renews our soul, restores our hope and ensures that our dreams are recaptured and realized.

NUGGETS OF INSPIRATION—*YOUR DESTINY AWAITS*

WITH GOD'S GREAT help, you can walk the Inner Path to True Greatness.

Through many dangers, toils, and snares
I have already come
'Tis Grace hath brought me safe thus far
And Grace will lead me home.
Amazing Grace
How sweet the sound.

—John Newton

The most important step you'll ever take to responsibly and confidently shape your destiny is the first—a serious commitment to the principles and values of Eternal Truth.

Let each become all that they were created capable of being.
—Thomas Carlyle

Being content with life means knowing God's purpose and plan for our lives, accepting them and cheerfully and joyfully working to fulfill them.

Faith is simply the welcome of the one who says, "Here I am." And taking that as our starting point, we can be on our way.

—Jacques Ellul

The Spirit of God is the Light on the path where we should go. It gives us courage, guides our steps as we travel it and imparts clear vision and sure Hope concerning where the journey will lead.

The exceptional life is the one connected at the heart to the Divine.

Our life is a special gift from above. What we do with it is our gift back.

We have a right to be happy and peaceful. We have been created for this—we are born to be happy—and we can only find true happiness and peace when we are in love with God.
—Mother Teresa

ABOUT THE AUTHOR

Cecil O. Kemp Jr. grew up on a small farm in rural Mississippi. He and Patty, his childhood sweetheart, have been married almost thirty years. Their two children have twice made the Kemps doting grandparents.

In 1971, Cecil graduated college, and began his professional career as a CPA working with one of the world's largest accounting firms. At twenty-three, he became chief financial officer of a public company and before thirty, became its chief operating officer.

Since 1982, the Kemps have owned and operated many successful businesses.

As a result of lessons learned from Cecil's near-fatal accident in 1993 and introspection on his father's unexpected death in 1995, Cecil and Patty have focused their energy full-time on sharing the message of Hope featured in all of Cecil's books and expressed in the products and services provided through their companies, the Wisdom Company and HopeStore.com. Their vision is to lead a renaissance of personal and workplace behavior shaped by the precepts of the Philosophy of Wisdom and its traditional values and priorities.

The Hope Collection is a series of beautiful, full-color gift books, based on Cecil's concepts and writings. These offer hope, encouragement, wisdom and inspiration to a variety of audiences, including students, new mothers, parents, leaders, those going through storms of life, and those in their retirement years.